"*God is God and I'm Not* presents the profound truth of God's sovereignty with a clear and compelling perspective on its life-transforming practicality. Dr. Witmer draws on his lifetime of ministry as a pastor and a discipler of pastors to lay the biblical foundation of the doctrine that God completely controls everything that happens in his universe and in our lives. He demonstrates that this reality, so humbling to our pride, is marvelously good news. He blends examples of biblical saints and contemporary believers who, amid storms, suffering, sorrow, and injustice, have found comfort, hope, and courage in their sovereign God. With patience and clarity, we are shown why God's sovereignty, mysterious as it is to our finite minds, does not negate our responsibility or excuse our sin or sluggishness. This book beautifully exemplifies how practical true theology is, amid daily challenges to our faith and endurance."

—Dr. Dennis E. Johnson
Professor Emeritus of Practical Theology,
Westminster Seminary California, Escondido, Calif.

"This book is an invitation 'to join the happy ranks of sovereigntists,' to believe that God is God and, as such, He is sovereign over all things. Dr. Witmer so ably shows us, first, that it's decidedly biblical to be a sovereigntist. Second, it's overwhelmingly practical, as Dr. Witmer shows us how only a sovereigntist view can help people effectively weather the storms and seasons of life. Count me among the members of the happy ranks, and I hope this book adds many, many more."

—Dr. Stephen J. Nichols
President, Reformation Bible College
Teaching Fellow, Ligonier Ministries

"The doctrine of the sovereignty of God is a tonic when things around us seem haphazard and often hostile. The truth that God holds the universe in the palm of His hands and orders the course of events from beginning to end helps us sleep at night and awake knowing that even when we sleep, He is in absolute control. Let Dr. Witmer reassure you again of God's sovereignty in all of life's vicissitudes, and you will be wonderfully blessed. I know no other book that will both inform and challenge you on this important truth, written with such ease and simplicity. I thoroughly commend it to you."

—Dr. Derek W.H. Thomas
Teaching Fellow, Ligonier Ministries
Chancellor's Professor of Systematic and Pastoral Theology
Reformed Theological Seminary

God Is God and I'm Not

God Is God and I'm Not

How God's Sovereignty Matters Every Day

TIMOTHY Z. WITMER

LIGONIER MINISTRIES

God Is God and I'm Not: How God's Sovereignty Matters Every Day

Published by Ligonier Ministries
421 Ligonier Court, Sanford, FL 32771
Ligonier.org

Printed in China
Dream Colour
0000925
First printing

ISBN 978-1-64289-709-8 (Hardcover)
ISBN 978-1-64289-710-4 (ePub)

Cover design: Ben Lueders and Ligonier Creative
Interior design and typeset: Katherine Lloyd, The DESK

Library of Congress Control Number: 2024952230

This book is dedicated, with thanksgiving to God,
to the congregations whom I have had the privilege of serving
on staff positions throughout fifty years of gospel ministry

First Baptist Church
Downingtown, Pa.
Youth Director: 1974–78

Springton Lake (formerly Berith) Presbyterian Church PCA)
Newtown Square, Pa.
Associate Pastor: 1979–86

Crossroads Community Church (PCA)
Upper Darby, Pa.
Pastor: 1986–2013

St. Stephen Reformed Church (PCA)
New Holland, Pa.
Pastor: 2014–21

Reformed Presbyterian Church (PCA)
Ephrata, Pa.
Interim Pastor: 2023–24

Soli Deo gloria

Contents

Part Four
That's a Good Question

Foreword

Later in these pages, you will discover that because God is God and Tim Witmer is not, he did not become the greatest and most famous tuba soloist ever seen on the stages of the great concert halls of the world. But for all I know, he may be the greatest tuba-playing professor of practical theology in the United States, and perhaps in the whole world. But even if he isn't, he is still a skilled musician, and more importantly, he has been an outstanding professor of practical theology, a wonderful pastor, and a great friend to me.

Reading his dedication page of *God is God and I'm Not*, I realize that we have enjoyed no less than forty years of friendship, ever since I made my way through the darkness of a Philadelphia winter's night to preach in Berith Presbyterian Church, where he was serving in the early 1980s. Ever since then, our friendship has grown through conferences shared when he played with the Westminster Brass, preaching in the churches he has pastored, and serving as colleagues at Westminster Theological Seminary. And because of that, I have had the opportunity to experience for myself what every reader of this book needs to know about its author: he is "the real deal," "the complete package." I don't mean that he is perfect in the sense of being sin-free. But he is at least in one sense of the word Scripture sometimes uses—he is a mature, well-rounded Christian, and he is an experienced and skilled pastor and pastoral theologian.

All of this you will experience for yourself as you begin to read *God is God and I'm Not.* It will make you want to be what Tim calls a "sovereigntist." That is a new word to me. The *Oxford English Dictionary* tells me it has been used to describe a person who believes in Quebec's right to self government, but I suspect Tim is the first person to make it a *theological* term! But I like it, and mean to start using it. I want to be one. And after reading these pages, I think you will, too.

The title says it all. It may remind you of some of Martin Luther's sayings. He once told the great Dutch scholar Desiderius Erasmus that his God was "too man-like"! And, of course, he more than once urged us to "let God be God!"

That is what it means to be a sovereigntist. And as Tim explains and applies the biblical teaching on God's sovereignty, I suspect readers will be helped in a variety of ways.

Some Christians are allergic to talk about God's sovereignty—for various reasons. Sometimes it is because others have misshaped their thinking. Other times, it is because they fear losing control of their own lives. Still other times, it is simply that they have never really taken in the fact that when the early Christians in Jerusalem prayed in a time of crisis, their first words were "Sovereign Lord" (Acts 4:24). In these pages, Dr. Witmer very graciously helps dissolve some of these personal, spiritual and theological hang-ups. To give you foretaste: occasionally, people object to teaching on God's sovereignty by using what they think of as a logical "defeater": "If God is sovereign, why pray?" Tim Witmer's gentle response? The truth is the reverse: "If God is not sovereign, what point is there in praying to Him?" You will need to read on to let him tell you more.

But this is not just another book arguing for the sovereignty of God. True, it is a work of theology. But it is theology of the best sort. It is biblical theology—the kind that makes a practical difference to our lives. Just glance through the table of contents page and you will see that. The seasons of life that Tim mentions are the very seasons that all of us experience. The challenges that he discusses are the challenges that we face. The questions that he answers are the questions that we ask. And all the way through, it will be clear to you that Tim and Barbara Witmer have "been there, done that, asked that, handled that"—and if not in exactly the same way that we have, it is clear that they have ministered to people just like us. Being present with Tim and Barbara in the churches that he has pastored and with the students whom he has taught is itself a confirmation that people respond to those who love them, care for them, and nourish and nurture them through all the seasons of life.

Tim Witmer's teaching on being an undershepherd to God's flock is well known among pastors. In one sense, this book is a natural next step. In it, he is not giving instruction to fellow pastors *about* being a pastor; he is being a pastor himself. I hope that many younger ministers will model themselves after the atmosphere of ministry in this book as well as its teaching. It will help them recalibrate their ministry to the foundational principle that Paul enunciated to Timothy: "The aim of our charge is love that issues from a pure heart and a good conscience and a sincere faith" (1 Tim. 1:5). And I can think of no greater compliment to pay to my friend as a pastor than that he has exemplified this in his own ministry. And if I can develop Paul's thought a little more broadly, since it is also true that "the aim of Christian friendship is love that issues from a pure heart and a good conscience and a sincere faith," then I can truly say that Timothy Witmer has modeled that to me.

You are in safe hands here. So take your time. Settle down with these pages. Read them thoughtfully (the reflection questions at the end of each chapter will help you do that). And in the process, learn from Tim Witmer's wise biblical teaching on what it means to be a sovereigntist.

—Sinclair B. Ferguson

Introduction

Some time ago, I was sitting in a waiting room of a well-known teaching hospital with a family, awaiting the results of the biopsy of their three-year-old daughter's newly discovered malignant brain tumor. This was a family who sensed that they had lost control of their lives. Everything had changed when they learned the jarring diagnosis. While they were doing all they could to care for their daughter, their future was filled with uncertainty. How could there be any comfort at all? Where was God in all this?

Many unforeseen circumstances come crashing into our lives. When they do, we lose a sense of control and hope. A truth that is essential to embrace if we are to navigate the storms of life is the doctrine of the sovereignty of God. Far from being an abstract theological doctrine, belief in God's lordship over all of life can make all the difference in how we live through hardship. And it is also important to embrace this truth in order to appreciate the greatest blessing when things are going well.

My objective is to help you find hope and help in your times of deepest need by anchoring you in the only place where such help can be found: the foundational truth of the sovereignty of God. I want to encourage you to become a *sovereigntist* (a word I coined in its theological sense, as far as I know): not simply a believer in this truth but someone who lives life in the light and power of the One who is Lord.

I came to embrace this truth as a new Christian during my freshman year in college. Reading the Bible was new to me, and I could already see clearly that the pages of Scripture heralded this doctrine. I didn't know that there was a special name for it, let alone a name for those who believed it. Soon I learned that my viewpoint was often referred to as *Calvinism* and that I was therefore a Calvinist, named for John Calvin, a sixteenth-century pastor and theologian who, along with many of the other Reformers, embraced this doctrine. Because of its connection with the Protestant Reformation, this perspective has also been called *Reformed theology*. Yet this doctrine did not originate with the Reformers but was revived alongside other truths with the return to the Scriptures. If that's what people who believed this scriptural doctrine were called, that was fine with me.

Michael Horton has noted that "both his [Calvin's] views and his impact are often exaggerated by friend and foe alike. For example, he is celebrated or vilified for his doctrine of predestination, despite the fact that he didn't have such a 'doctrine'—at least in terms of a unique view or emphasis. There's nothing in Calvin's teaching on predestination that isn't also found in the great stream of Augustinian teaching."[1] As you will see, its origin is in the Scriptures, and it has been carried to us through the centuries by those who have embraced the authority of the Bible, including John Calvin. Though Calvin is the name that is most often associated with this doctrine, those of us who embrace the scriptural truth of the reign and rule of God over all things should rightly be called *sovereigntists* and not *Calvinists*. Many

1 Michael Horton, "What's So Special about John Calvin?," Crossway.org, March 21, 2014, https://www.crossway.org/articles/whats-so-special-about-john-calvin/.

have famously observed that Calvin wrote more extensively on prayer and the Holy Spirit than predestination. J.A. Medders noted that

> Calvin taught much more than Calvinism. In his day, he would have scoffed at the idea of an "-ism" being tethered to his name. In the *Institutes of the Christian Religion*—his major work of theology—you'll find more pages devoted to prayer, baptism, and the Lord's Supper than to election.[2]

Concerning this book, my hope is that it will help you stand unshaken (or less shaken) when the inevitable waves of trouble come crashing down so that you will be able to sincerely say, "God is God and I'm not!"

Now for a few words about the structure of the book. Chapters 1 and 2 constitute part 1, "Firm Foundations." Though this is not largely a theological work, chapter 1 will introduce you to the doctrine of the sovereignty of God and some important terminology that is commonly used but often confusing and misunderstood. Chapter 2 will introduce you to the foundational promise found in Romans 8:28, a comprehensive promise that could not be true if God were not sovereign. Part 2 is called "Seasons of Life under God's Sovereign Care," in which we see how the truth of God's sovereignty helps in the different seasons and circumstances of life, including the good times and the bad times. The last two parts comprise chapters that address challenges and questions that come to mind. Each chapter includes a "Mark" that should characterize sovereigntists. Finally, every chapter will end with a few reflection questions.

2 J.A. Medders, *Humble Calvinism* (n.p.: Good Book, 2019), 33–34.

Within these chapters, you will find real-life vignettes or biblical illustrations that demonstrate how belief in the sovereignty of God can make all the difference between despair and hope. I pray that this little book will help you walk through the seasons of life trusting in our great sovereign God and that you will find the kind of comfort and encouragement in this great truth that Charles Hodge describes:

> The sovereignty of God is the ground of peace and confidence to all his people. They rejoice that the Lord God omnipotent reigneth; that neither necessity, nor chance, nor the folly of man, nor the malice of Satan controls the sequence of events and all their issues. Infinite wisdom, love, and power, belong to Him, our great God and Savior, into whose hands all power in heaven and earth has been committed.[3]

John Calvin's favorite verse was Deuteronomy 29:29: "The secret things belong to the LORD our God, but the things that are revealed belong to us and to our children forever, that we may do all the words of this law." There are indeed many secret things and mysteries to us about God's plan, but His Word reveals more than enough to direct and comfort us until we meet Him face-to-face.

---

3 Charles Hodge, *Systematic Theology*, vol. 1 (Grand Rapids, Mich.: Eerdmans, 1975), 441.

Part One

FIRM FOUNDATIONS

1

"God Is God and I'm Not"

Introduction to the Doctrine of the Sovereignty of God

"Our God is in the heavens; he does all that he pleases."
(Ps. 115:3)

Sure, it's easy to *say,* "God is God and I'm not," acknowledging the absolute reign of God, but what does the statement really mean? If you are going to be a committed sovereigntist, you need to know what it means to say that God is sovereign. Rather than a comprehensive survey of the biblical doctrine of the sovereignty of God, this chapter is intended to be an introduction that will lay the groundwork on which we can build the practical implications of His reign in our lives.

To Say That "God Is God" Is to Say That God Is Sovereign

To be *sovereign* is to exercise "supreme rank, power, or authority."[1] Of course, there are earthly sovereigns, kings, queens, presidents, and

1 Dictionary.com, s.v. "sovereign," http://dictionary.reference.com/browse/sovereign?s=t.

prime ministers, but their reigns cannot compare with the reign of the Lord. Louis Berkhof provides this summary:

> He is clothed with absolute authority over the hosts of heaven and the inhabitants of the earth. He upholds all things with His almighty power, and determines the end to which they are destined to serve. He rules as King in the most absolute sense of the word, and all things are dependent on Him and subservient to Him.[2]

This concept is beautifully expressed in these words of David: "Yours is the kingdom, O LORD, and you are exalted as head above all. Both riches and honor come from you, and you rule over all" (1 Chron. 29:11–12). Arthur Pink authored a classic work on the sovereignty of God, and in it he explains:

> The Sovereignty of God. What do we mean by this expression? We mean the supremacy of God, the kingship of God, the godhood of God. To say that God is Sovereign is to declare that God is God. To say that God is Sovereign is to declare that He is the Most High, doing according to His will in the army of Heaven, and among the inhabitants of the earth, so that none can stay His hand or say unto Him what doest Thou? (Dan. 4:35). To say that God is Sovereign is to declare that He is the Almighty, the Possessor of all power in Heaven and earth, so that none can defeat His counsels, thwart His purpose, or resist His will (Psa. 115:3). To say that God is Sovereign is to declare that He is "The Governor among the nations"

---

2 Louis Berkhof, *Systematic Theology* (Grand Rapids, Mich.: Eerdmans, 1976), 76.

> (Psa. 22:28), setting up kingdoms, overthrowing empires, and determining the course of dynasties as pleaseth Him best. To say that God is Sovereign is to declare that He is the "Only Potentate, the King of kings, and Lord of lords." (1 Tim. 6:15)[3]

That is quite a statement, so let's take a moment to unpack the comprehensiveness of God's reign.

He Reigns Everywhere

We begin by acknowledging that there would be no "everywhere" apart from the fact that God created the heavens and the earth. This truth is proclaimed from Genesis to Revelation. The Scriptures open with these words: "In the beginning, God created the heavens and the earth" (Gen. 1:1). In the last book of the Bible, the same theme is sounded by the assembly in heaven: "Worthy are you, our Lord and God, to receive glory and honor and power, for you created all things, and by your will they existed and were created" (Rev. 4:11).

At one time, it could be said that "the sun never set" on the British Empire because of its presence on every inhabited continent. That was quite a vast empire indeed. Yet the Lord reigns *everywhere*, not only on this planet but over the entire universe! "Let the heavens be glad, and let the earth rejoice, and let them say among the nations, 'The LORD reigns!'" (1 Chron. 16:31). There is no place over which He does not reign: "The LORD has established his throne in the heavens, and his kingdom rules over all" (Ps. 103:19). D.A. Carson writes, "His sovereignty extends over the mighty movements of the

3 Arthur W. Pink, *The Sovereignty of God* (London: Banner of Truth, 1968), 20.

stars in their courses, over the fall of a sparrow, over the exact count of the hairs of my head."[4]

Not only did God create all things, but He sustains them as well. When the Apostle Paul addressed the Athenian philosophers on Mars Hill, he combined the concepts of God as Creator and God as Sustainer of all: "And he made from one man every nation of mankind to live on all the face of the earth, having determined allotted periods and the boundaries of their dwelling place, that they should seek God, and perhaps feel their way toward him and find him. Yet he is actually not far from each one of us, for 'In him we live and move and have our being'" (Acts 17:26–28).

This means that God's right of rule extends over your life, your home, and your workplace. There is no place where you or a loved one can be out of His view.

He Reigns All the Time

Human sovereigns rule for a limited period of time. In the United States, for example, an individual can hold the presidency for only two terms. There are no term limits on God! In some nations, leaders may rule a lot longer. For example, Queen Elizabeth II reigned over the United Kingdom for seventy years. Louis XIV bested her by two years. But the Scriptures teach that the Lord reigns *forever*: "The LORD will reign forever and ever" (Ex. 15:18). It can't be put more plainly than that. There was never a time that He did not reign, and there will never be a time when His reign comes to an end: "You, O LORD, are on high forever" (Ps. 92:8). He never takes

4 D.A. Carson, *The Difficult Doctrine of the Love of God* (Wheaton, Ill.: Crossway, 2000), 49.

a nap, either: "Behold, he who keeps Israel will neither slumber nor sleep" (Ps. 121:4). The great result is that He is caring for us *all the time*. "It is in vain that you rise up early and go late to rest, eating the bread of anxious toil; for he gives to his beloved sleep" (Ps. 127:2). The psalmist's message is that there is no need to stay up worrying or to lose sleep over things because the Lord is always watching out for you. He is with you all the time. He is working out His plans in the good times and in the bad times.

He Reigns over Everything, Including Me

God not only creates and sustains but also determines the course of history and the course of our lives. In his letter to the Ephesians, Paul writes that the Lord "works all things according to the counsel of his will" (Eph. 1:11). After enduring unimaginable suffering, the futile attempts of his friends to provide comfort, and the Lord's rebuke, Job exclaimed, "I know that you can do all things, and that no purpose of yours can be thwarted" (Job 42:2). The psalmist declared, "Our God is in the heavens; he does all that he pleases" (Ps. 115:3). Wise King Solomon spoke of His reign when he wrote: "I perceived that whatever God does endures forever; nothing can be added to it, nor anything taken from it. God has done it, so that people fear before him" (Eccl. 3:14).

Before going any further, it will be beneficial to define some terms in order to unpack this important subject.

A Glossary of God's Sovereignty

My prayer is that these definitions will be simple without being simplistic. Granted, this is quite a challenge when tackling such lofty subjects, but here goes. The sovereignty of God is often thought of as an *attribute* of God alongside His omniscience (He is all-knowing), His omnipotence (He is all-powerful), and His omnipresence (He is present everywhere). These attributes, together with many others, exist in the being of God and together express His glory!

But God's sovereignty is *above*, rather than alongside, His attributes. This is how theologian Charles Hodge explains it: "Sovereignty is not a property of the divine nature but a prerogative arising out of the perfections of the Supreme Being."[5] This means that the exercise and demonstration of His attributes is according to His sovereign purpose. According to Pink: "Sovereignty characterizes the whole Being of God. He is sovereign in all His attributes."[6] For example, He sovereignly exercises His power, He sovereignly exercises His mercy, and so on. John Frame summarizes God's sovereignty by saying, "The sovereignty of God is the same as the *lordship* of God, for God is the *sovereign* over all of creation."[7]

And God's sovereignty is not a passive reign. It is exercised in "determining whatsoever comes to pass." This is the necessary consequence if God's reign is truly comprehensive. R.C. Sproul makes the point that it is a necessary consequence of theism. He once asked a class how many of them believed that "God from all eternity," according to His own holy and wise counsel, did "freely and immutably ordain, or foreordain, whatsoever comes to pass." Many put their hands up. Then he asked whether those who had not raised their

---

5 Charles Hodge, *Systematic Theology*, vol. 1 (Grand Rapids, Mich.: Eerdmans, 1975), 440.

6 Pink, *Sovereignty of God*, 22.

7 John M. Frame, "The Sovereignty of God," The Gospel Coalition, https://www.thegospelcoalition.org/essay/the-sovereignty-of-god/ (emphasis original).

hands were atheists. Of course, those students were shocked by that conclusion. Here's how Sproul recounts the rest of the interaction:

> I was saying, "Because, if you don't believe this statement, you understand that fundamentally, at the bottom line, you're an atheist." And that was about the most outrageous thing they ever heard in their lives. I said, "Well, let's understand that this statement that I've just read, that God has foreordained whatsoever comes to pass, is not a statement that is unique to Calvinism or to Presbyterianism. It doesn't distinguish the Reformed tradition from other traditions. It doesn't even distinguish Christians from Jews or from Muslims. This statement here distinguishes theists from atheists." And they were still puzzled as I continued this harangue. And I said, "Don't you see? If there's anything that happens in this world outside the foreordination of God—if there's no sense in which God is ordaining whatsoever comes to pass—then at whatever point something happens outside the foreordination of God it is, therefore, happening outside of the sovereignty of God."[8]

The conclusion is clear. If God does not ordain whatsoever comes to pass, He is not God.

Let's launch into some other terms that help us understand God's reign. We will continue to build this graphic as we move through the rest of this chapter:

---

8 R.C. Sproul, "God Ordains Whatsoever Comes to Pass," Ligonier.org, March 17, 2021, https://www.ligonier.org/posts/god-ordains-whatsoever-comes-pass.

Sovereignty
(His lordship)

|

God's Decree
(His master plan)

Not all terms are explicitly used in the Bible, but they describe important scriptural principles of His divine reign. One such word is the *decree* of God. In summary, the decree of God (often made plural: *decrees*) is His sovereign *plan*.[9]

One of the most remarkable products of the Reformation is the collection of Westminster Standards.[10] Here are the opening words of the third chapter of the Westminster Confession of Faith that summarize this great truth: "God, from all eternity, did, by the most wise and holy counsel of his own will, freely, and unchangeably ordain whatsoever comes to pass: yet so, as thereby neither is God the author of sin, nor is violence offered to the will of the creatures; nor is the liberty or contingency of second causes taken away, but rather established." As with any other good doctrinal statement, there are affirmations and denials. What is affirmed is that God ordains "whatsoever comes to pass." This is known as the sovereign decree of God. Question and answer 7 of the Westminster Shorter

9 Berkhof notes, "Though we often speak of the decrees of God in the plural, yet in its own nature the divine decree is but a single act of God." Berkhof, *Systematic Theology* (Grand Rapids, Mich.: Eerdmans, 1976), 102.

10 The Westminster Assembly was convened from 1643 to 1653 and consisted of more than 120 ministers. They produced a Form of Government, a Directory of Public Worship, the Westminster Confession of Faith, and the Larger and Shorter Catechisms.

Catechism give a precise definition of the decrees of God: "What are the decrees of God?" Answer: "The decrees of God are, his eternal purpose, according to the counsel of his will, whereby, for his own glory, he hath foreordained whatsoever comes to pass."

To clarify the use of singular *decree* and plural *decrees*, Hodge notes:

> The decrees of God are all reducible to one purpose. By this is meant that from the indefinite number of systems, or series of possible events, present to the divine mind, God determined on the futurition or actual occurrence of the existing order of things, with all its changes, minute as well as great, from the beginning of time to all eternity. The reason, therefore, why any event occurs, or, that it passes from the possible into that of the actual, is that God has so decreed. The decrees of God, therefore, are not many, but one purpose.[11]

John Piper comments: "The purposes of God cannot be frustrated: there is none like God. If a purpose of God came to naught, it would imply that there is a power greater than God's. It would imply that someone could stay His hand when He designs to do a thing."[12] C.S. Lewis observes that "no cause other than Himself produces His acts and no external obstacle impedes them—that His own goodness is the root from which they all grow and His own omnipotence the air in which they all flower."[13] So think of the decree of God as His master plan.

---

11 Hodge, *Systematic Theology*, 1:537.

12 John Piper, *Desiring God*, rev. ed. (Colorado Springs, Colo.: Multnomah, 2011), 33.

13 C.S. Lewis, *The Problem of Pain* (1940; repr., New York: HarperOne, 1996), 17.

Sovereignty
(His lordship)

|

God's Decree
(His master plan)

|

Providence
(overseeing the outworking of His plan in time)

Stay with me now. Sovereignty is the *lordship* of God, the *decree* is the plan of God, and next we come to another important word: *providence*. If the decree is God's eternal plan, providence is God's carrying out and overseeing the execution of that plan in the world. Berkhof notes, "A distinction must be made between the decree and its execution."[14] This idea is beautifully expressed in question and answer 27 of the Heidelberg Catechism:

Q. What do you understand by the providence of God?

A. Providence is
the almighty and ever present power of God
by which God upholds, as with his hand,
heaven
and earth
and all creatures,
and so rules them that
leaf and blade,

14 Berkhof, *Systematic Theology*, 107.

rain and drought,
fruitful and lean years,
food and drink,
health and sickness,
prosperity and poverty—
all things, in fact, come to us
not by chance
but by his fatherly hand.

In these words you can see a distinction between God's providential work in upholding nature and humanity, as we see in our additions to the tree of sovereignty vocabulary:

Providence and the Natural World

The Scriptures affirm in several places not only God's creative power but also His ongoing sovereignty over the natural world. One such text is Psalm 104. His creative power is seen in verse 5, "He set the earth on its foundations, so that it should never be moved," and in verse 8, "The mountains rose, the valleys sank down to the place that you appointed for them."

Much of the rest of the psalm is given to the description of God's providential care over nature. It speaks of vegetation:

> You cause the grass to grow for the livestock
> and plants for man to cultivate,
> that he may bring forth food from the earth
> and wine to gladden the heart of man,
> oil to make his face shine
> and bread to strengthen man's heart. (vv. 14–15)

It includes His direction of the heavenly bodies:

> He made the moon to mark the seasons;
> the sun knows its time for setting.
> You make darkness, and it is night,
> when all the beasts of the forest creep about. (vv. 19–20)

A wonderful summary of His sovereign plan over nature is seen in the following verses:

> Whatever the LORD pleases, he does,
> in heaven and on earth,
> in the seas and all deeps.
> He it is who makes the clouds rise at the end of the earth,
> who makes lightnings for the rain
> and brings forth the wind from his storehouses. (Ps. 135:6–7)

Providence and Humanity

The working out of God's providential plan for humanity is also described in the Bible. For example, in the Apostle Paul's sermon on Mars Hill in Athens, he said:

> And he made from one man every nation of mankind to live on all the face of the earth, having determined allotted periods and the boundaries of their dwelling place, that they should seek God, and perhaps feel their way toward him and find him. Yet he is actually not far from each one of us, for
>
> "In him we live and move and have our being." (Acts 17:26–28)

These words speak of the origin of humanity but also include the assertion that the places and times of our existence have been determined by the Lord. Why were you born *when* you were born? Why were you born *where* you were born? Both are part of God's plan.

The scope of God's providence is also seen in Psalm 139:

> For you formed my inward parts;
> you knitted me together in my mother's womb.
> I praise you, for I am fearfully and wonderfully made.
> Wonderful are your works;
> my soul knows it very well.
> My frame was not hidden from you,
> when I was being made in secret,
> intricately woven in the depths of the earth.
> Your eyes saw my unformed substance;
> in your book were written, every one of them,

the days that were formed for me,
when as yet there was none of them. (vv. 13–16)

From the moment of conception through the very last day of your life, the Lord's plan is unfolding. This includes the promise to guide you and to provide for your needs.

Though the distinction can be made between God's providence in natural creation and His providence with respect to humanity, *providence* generally refers to God's directing the outworking of His plan over all. This can be seen in our addition to the tree of terminology:

Now we come to another word that has been the subject of lots of theological debate and late-night college-dorm discussions, too. When we introduce you to the terminology of sovereignty, we have to talk about the elephant in the room: *predestination*. This *is* a biblical word, as we will see in a moment. For some, *predestination* is another way of saying that "God ordains everything that comes to pass." So sometimes the term is used as a synonym for the decree of God or for the providence of God, but most often it is used to describe God's sovereignty over His plan of salvation. Berkhof notes that "in distinction from the decree of God *in general*, predestination has reference to God's rational creatures only. Most frequently, it refers to fallen men."[15]

Let's see where this fits into the overall picture. *Sovereignty* is God's lordship, the *decree* is His plan, and *providence* is His working out that plan; then *predestination* describes the exercise of His sovereignty over the matter of salvation.

Please note that this was not merely John Calvin's view. "The Reformers of the sixteenth century all advocated the strictest doctrine of predestination."[16] But we would not advocate this concept if it were not clearly taught in the Scriptures. Paul writes that in Christ "we have obtained an inheritance, having been predestined according to the purpose of him who works all things according to the counsel of his will" (Eph. 1:11). He also writes to the Romans that "those whom he foreknew he also predestined to be conformed to the image of his Son, in order that he might be the firstborn among many brothers" (Rom. 8:29). So the language of predestination applies to the question of salvation. Here is how it appears on our sovereignty tree of terminology:

---

15 Berkhof, 113 (emphasis original).

16 Berkhof, 110.

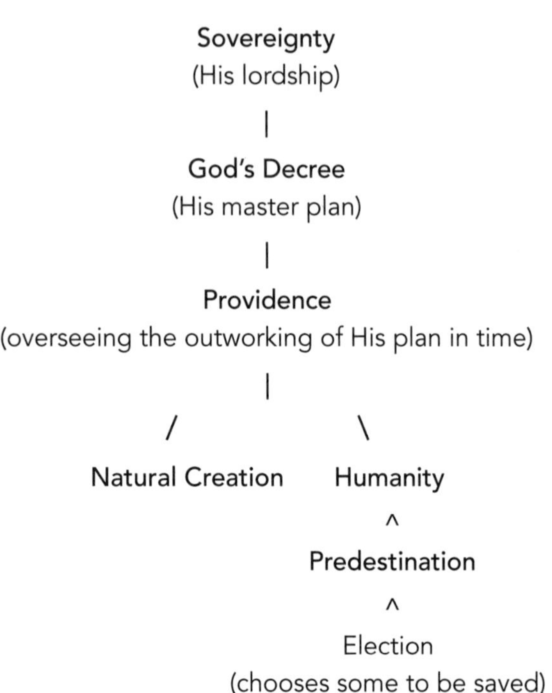

Another important word in the glossary of sovereignty, therefore, is *election*. It answers the question of how God exercises His sovereignty in order to save sinners. It expresses the fact that part of the exercise of God's sovereignty is that He "elects" or chooses some to be saved. This is an undeniable product of His sovereign reign. I was about to write that it is a *necessary* exercise of His lordship, but this would not be accurate. It was not *necessary* for God to display His mercy to rebellious and disobedient humanity. To save anyone is strictly the fruit of His grace and love.

The fact that God has graciously exercised His sovereign choice is evident from the very beginning of the biblical narrative. He chose

Abel and not Cain; He chose Abraham to whom to give the covenant promises; He chose Isaac and not Ishmael; He chose Jacob and not Esau. He also chose Israel among all the nations of the earth to be His people, through whom would come forth the promised Messiah.

Why did God choose Israel? The answer is found in Deuteronomy 7: "For you are a people holy to the LORD your God. The LORD your God has chosen you to be a people for his treasured possession, out of all the peoples who are on the face of the earth. It was not because you were more in number than any other people that the LORD set his love on you and chose you, for you were the fewest of all peoples, but it is because the LORD loves you and is keeping the oath that he swore to your fathers" (vv. 6–8). Notice that the motivation for His choice is found in another attribute: love. Paul brings it all together when he reminds the Ephesian church that "he chose us in him before the foundation of the world, that we should be holy and blameless before him. In love he predestined us for adoption to himself as sons through Jesus Christ, according to the purpose of his will, to the praise of his glorious grace, with which he has blessed us in the Beloved" (Eph. 1:4–6).

Jesus also taught His disciples, "You did not choose me, but I chose you and appointed you that you should go and bear fruit and that your fruit should abide, so that whatever you ask the Father in my name, he may give it to you" (John 15:16). The salvation of sinful human beings has nothing to do with my merit, my works, or my worthiness. It is strictly a gift of God's grace. In the second chapter of his letter to the Ephesians, Paul wrote: "For by grace you have been saved through faith. And this is not your own doing; it is the gift of God, not a result of works, so that no one may boast" (Eph. 2:8–9).

But what about the question of those whom God does not save?

This brings us to another important word in the glossary of sovereignty: *reprobation*.

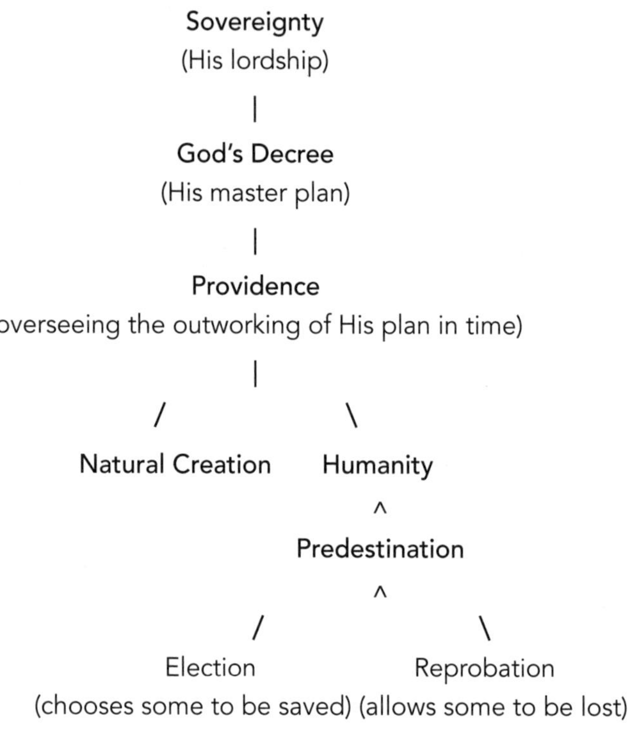

The doctrine of reprobation speaks of the fact that while God is *able* to save all, He chooses to save only some and allow others to suffer the consequences of their sin. While this sounds "unfair" to our ears, we must remember that God would have been perfectly just in allowing *the entire human race* to be condemned because of our sinfulness. Imagine that all of us are hurtling down the Niagara River toward the great falls (remembering that we are in this situation only because we jumped into the river despite warnings about the dangers ahead). We are all speeding toward the judgment that we deserve, but God plucks some out of the river by His grace and saves them.

Why doesn't God save everyone? This is a mystery, but it is His prerogative as the sovereign Lord. Anticipating an objection to God's choice of Jacob over Esau, Paul writes: "What shall we say then? Is there injustice on God's part? By no means! For he says to Moses, 'I will have mercy on whom I have mercy, and I will have compassion on whom I have compassion.' So then it depends not on human will or exertion, but on God, who has mercy" (Rom. 9:14–16). Berkhof observes: "We can only say that God passed some by for good and wise reasons sufficient to Himself. On the other hand, the reason for condemnation is known: it is sin."[17]

While some might find this truth to be troubling, it provides comfort and peace to those who love the Lord. Alexander Carson notes, "Nothing can be more consoling to the man of God, than the conviction that the Lord who made the world governs the world; and that every event, great and small, prosperous and adverse, is under the absolute disposal of Him who doth all things well, and who regulates all things for the good of his people."[18]

What about Human Responsibility?

In terms of the "denials" of the Westminster Confession, as we will see in subsequent chapters, focusing on the doctrine of the sovereignty of God does not preclude or replace human agency: "Neither is God the author of sin, nor is violence offered to the will of the creatures; nor is the liberty or contingency of second causes taken

17 Berkhof, 116.

18 Quoted in Jerry Bridges, *The Practice of Godliness* (Carol Stream, Ill.: NavPress, 1996), 214.

away, but rather established" (WCF 3.1). Pink writes, "To emphasize the sovereignty of God, without also maintaining the accountability of the creature, tends to fatalism; to be so concerned in maintaining the responsibilities of man, as to lose sight of the sovereign God, is to exalt the creature and dishonour the Creator."[19]

Scripture assures us that God's sovereignty and human beings' responsibility[20] are compatible assertions. Carson writes: "It does not claim to show you *how* they are compatible. It claims only that we can get far enough in the evidence and the arguments to show how they are not *in*compatible, and that it is therefore entirely reasonable to think they are compatible if there is good evidence for them."[21] He goes on to reference the disciples' words of praise in the wake of their persecution as a good example of their compatibility, "for truly in this city there were gathered together against your holy servant Jesus, whom you anointed, both Herod and Pontius Pilate, along with the Gentiles and the peoples of Israel, to do whatever your hand and your plan had predestined to take place" (Acts 4:27–28). It was foreordained that He should be betrayed, but woe to him who fulfilled the decree. Here foreordination and responsibility are by our Lord Himself declared to exist and to be consistent. Here, the sovereign plan of God is placed side by side with the responsibility of the human agents who put Jesus to death.

Yes, there is compatibility, though mysterious, between the sovereignty of God and humans' responsibility for their actions. No, the doctrine of God's reign, rightly understood, does not lead us to

19 Pink, *Sovereignty of God*, 9.

20 Hodge, *Systematic Theology*, 1:544.

21 Carson, *Difficult Doctrine of the Love of God*, 52, emphasis original.

fatalism, stoicism, or a *que será, será* approach to life. It is designed to provide comfort and encouragement to those who follow Him.

But Is God Really Sovereign?

Let's take one last look at the glossary of sovereignty terminology. Are you convinced that God is sovereign? Are you willing to say that "God is God and I'm not"? If not, with what would you replace His sovereignty? Would you put *chance* at the top of the tree? This is really the same as putting *nothing* there, and it provides little comfort as we walk through life. Would you replace it with a modified definition of God's sovereignty? How would you restrict His rule? Are there some things over which He reigns and others over which He does not? When we ask these questions, we are getting to the heart of the matter, aren't we? It is a lot easier to say "God is God" than to say "I'm not." When we place our opinions above the clearly revealed principles of God's Word, we are placing ourselves at the top of the tree, as king of the hill, in the position of lordship. Ah, it is the question whether God is sovereign over your life or *you are*. Isn't failing to say that "God is God and I'm not" declaring that "I am God and He's not" instead? This is the dilemma of the sinful human condition and represents the age-old struggle in the hearts and minds of fallen humanity.

But replacing "I am God" with "God is God" results in true peace and comfort. As A.W. Pink wrote: "It produces gratitude in prosperity and patience in adversity. It affords comfort for the present and a sense of security respecting the unknown future."[22]

---

22 A.W. Pink, *The Sovereignty of God* (1919; repr., London: I.C. Herendeen, 1968), 139.

There are certainly great mysteries and unanswered questions concerning this doctrine that must be left to the wisdom of God. This was the Apostle Paul's perspective as he brought his great exposition of the doctrine of predestination to its conclusion: "Oh, the depth of the riches and wisdom and knowledge of God! How unsearchable are his judgments and how inscrutable his ways! 'For who has known the mind of the Lord, or who has been his counselor?' 'Or who has given a gift to him that he might be repaid?' For from him and through him and to him are all things. To him be glory forever. Amen" (Rom. 11:33–36). In concluding his discussion with these words, the Apostle was saying, "God is God and I'm not."

Mark of a Sovereigntist: Humility

Since God is sovereign over all things, including our salvation, there is no room for boasting! If we have even a shadowy glimpse of the sovereign glory of God, it will compel us to fall on our faces in awe. Paul Tripp comments, "There is nothing that will put you in your place, nothing that will correct your distorted view of yourself, nothing that will yank you out of your functional arrogance, or nothing that will take the winds out of the sails of your self-righteousness like standing, without defense, before the awesome glory of God."[23]

Add to this hint of the realization of the awesome nature of God that He has given us the gifts of forgiveness and eternal life, gifts that we could never earn or deserve, and our jaws should drop! This is exactly what Paul concluded after his summary of God's gracious salvation: "For by grace you have been saved through faith. And this is

---

23 Paul David Tripp, *Dangerous Calling: Confronting the Unique Challenges of Pastoral Ministry* (Wheaton, Ill.: Crossway, 2012), 121.

not your own doing; it is the gift of God, not a result of works, so that no one may boast" (Eph. 2:8–9). This is a gift of God, not something achieved by our own doing or our own works. Therefore, no boasting! Don't forget that these gifts were earned through works. Not through *your* works, but through the life, death, and resurrection of His Son, Jesus Christ. John Stott remarks: "Every time we look at the cross Christ seems to say to us, 'I am here because of you. It is your sin I am bearing, your curse I am suffering, your debt I am paying, your death I am dying.' Nothing in history or in the universe cuts us down to size like the cross. All of us have inflated views of ourselves, especially in self-righteousness, until we have visited a place called Calvary. It is there, at the foot of the cross, that we shrink to our true size."[24]

No wonder these are "things into which angels long to look" (1 Peter 1:12).

For Further Reflection

1. Take a few minutes and consider the meaning and implications of the truth that God is sovereign.
2. Why do many people find this truth disturbing?
3. What are the alternatives to replace God's sovereignty at the top of the glossary graphic?
4. What are the consequences of the alternatives?
5. Why is humility an appropriate mark of the sovereigntist?

---

24 John R.W. Stott, *The Message of Galatians* (Downers Grove, Ill.: InterVarsity Press, 1968), 179.

2

A Sovereign Promise to Stand On

Romans 8:28

"And we know that for those who love God all things work together for good, for those who are called according to his purpose."
(Rom. 8:28)

You have been introduced to the terminology of sovereignty, so it is time to get into its practical implications. Here is where the rubber meets the road. If this is true, how does it affect your daily life? What does the life of the sovereigntist look like?

One of the most important steps in the application of this truth is to expand one's perspective from the horizonal, earthbound place where we live with most of our difficulties to include the vertical dimension of God's involvement in our lives. A primary means of accomplishing this is to search the Scriptures to see what God Himself says about these things. When we engage in such a search, we discover lots of encouragement, including the promises that He has made to His people.

One of the promises that is foundational to the life of the sovereigntist is the wonderful assurance found in the eighth chapter of Paul's letter to the Romans: "And we know that God causes all things to work together for good to those who love God, to those who are called according to His purpose" (Rom. 8:28, NASB). The heart of the promise is found in the words "*all things* work together for good" (ESV). Notice the comprehensiveness of this promise. It doesn't say that *some* things or *most* things, but *all* things work together for good. Can you see that God cannot make this promise unless He is in control of *everything*? I suppose He could *make* the promise, but He certainly couldn't *keep* it unless He were the Ruler of all things. In the course of our study, we will see what this looks like in many of the scenarios that we encounter in life.

You can also see that Romans 8:28 says not that all things *are* good, but that all things *work together for* good. This is where the mystery lies from our perspective. Many of the circumstances that we experience are not good, but in God's mysterious plan, they "turn out for the good." R.C. Sproul reminds us:

> If God is able to make everything that happens to us work together for our good, then ultimately everything that happens to us is good. We must be careful to stress here the word *ultimately*. On the earthly plane things that happen to us may indeed be evil. . . . Yet God in His goodness transcends all these things and works them out to our good. For the Christian, *ultimately*, there are no tragedies.[1]

---

1 R.C. Sproul, *Essential Truths of the Christian Faith* (Carol Stream, Ill.: Tyndale, 1992), 50, emphasis original.

This is a remarkable perspective, but if we really believe the promise, we must embrace this reality. John Murray adds: "Many of the things comprised are evil in themselves and it is the marvel of God's wisdom and grace that they, when taken in concert with the whole, are made to work for good. Not one detail works ultimately for evil to the people of God; in the end only good will be their lot."[2] Often, we have the joy of seeing this in hindsight, but not always. In some circumstances, we will not understand His plan in this lifetime. Nonetheless, His promise is true.

Earlier I mentioned that we need to expand our perspective from the things we are facing to include the vertical involvement of God. It is OK to say that the hardships we endure are *not* good. In fact, it is OK to say that many of them are *bad*. But this promise includes God in the equation; the bad things we are experiencing are mysteriously, providentially being used for our good. Sinclair Ferguson offers this perspective: "How can all things be worked together by God for good? The answer is at hand. It is because God's ultimate purpose is to make us like Christ. His goal is the complete restoration of the image of God in His child! So great a work demands all the resources which God finds throughout the universe, and He ransacks the possibilities of joys and sorrows in order to reproduce in us the character of Jesus."[3]

It must also be recognized that the Romans 8:28 promise is not a universal promise for all people. We are told that this promise is "to those who love God, to those who are called according to His

2 John Murray, *The Epistle to the Romans*, New International Commentary on the New Testament (Grand Rapids, Mich.: Eerdmans, 1959), 314.

3 Sinclair Ferguson, *The Christian Life* (Carlisle, Pa.: Banner of Truth, 1997), 21.

purpose." Jesus was once asked to identify the greatest commandment. He replied: "You shall love the Lord your God with all your heart and with all your soul and with all your mind. This is the great and first commandment" (Matt. 22:37–38). The problem is that loving God is not a natural condition for us. In fact, the Scriptures teach that just the opposite is true.

Earlier in Paul's letter, he reminds us, "None is righteous, no, not one; no one understands; no one seeks for God" (Rom. 3:10–11). We are also described as His "enemies" (5:10). But the whole point of the book of Romans is to show how the Lord sovereignly changes all this. The answer to how we are transformed from enemies of God to lovers of God is found in the phrase "for those who are called according to his purpose." This is made possible through the exercise of God's sovereign grace by sending His Son into the world to take upon Himself the punishment for our sins and in that "while we were enemies we were reconciled to God by the death of his Son" (5:10). Through faith in Jesus, our sins are forgiven, the barriers are removed, and "all the promises of God find their Yes in him" (2 Cor. 1:20). We love Him only because He first loved us.

But what is the calling that Paul mentions? Theologians describe this as the *effectual call*: the call to faith in the gospel that is made effectual by the Spirit's softening and opening our hearts to understand, believe, and receive. Sovereigntists must begin by recognizing that only by the Spirit's work in our hearts may our eyes be opened to the ugliness of our sin and the beauty of His work on our behalf.

Once again, the promise circles back to God's sovereignty when it refers to those who are "called according to *his purpose*" (emphasis added). The whole premise of the promise and, in fact, the premise of Paul's whole letter to the Roman church is that only by God's grace through faith in Jesus Christ can we be right with God. This is His ultimate purpose for His people within which this promise finds its anchor. According to Martin Luther, whose life was changed (and then the world!) through the study of this letter: "There is no other reason why the many tribulations and evils cannot separate believers from the love of God than that they are called 'according to his purpose.' Hence God makes all things work together for good to them, and to them only. If there would not be this divine purpose, but [if] our salvation would rest upon our will or work, it would be based on chance. How easily in that case could one single evil hinder or destroy it."[4]

He Works the Good and the Bad for Our Good

But we cannot limit the "good" only to our ultimate salvation. Douglas Moo writes: "Given the context, Paul undoubtedly thinks of our final salvation (see vv. 18, 30 [of Rom. 8]). However, we should probably not limit the good to our final glory only; it will also include the many blessings that God wants to give us in this life."[5] This is to say that not only does He cause "bad" things to work together for good, but He also causes "good" things to work together for good. Perhaps a clearer way to articulate this nuance is that God works the good things together for something better. For example, He might "work" the birth of a child (something good) together to draw the child's parents closer to each other (something better). Or one might receive a promotion (something good) to meet an unexpected

4 Martin Luther, *Commentary on Romans* (Grand Rapids, Mich.: Kregel, 1954), 128.

5 Douglas J. Moo, *Encountering the Book of Romans* (Grand Rapids, Mich.: Baker Academic, 2002), 140.

financial need (something better). But remember, as Moo writes, "Although all things that touch the life of a Christian are used by God for our good, that good will often be an ultimate spiritual good."[6] The remarkable truth is that He is working all things, good and bad, for our ultimate good. Thanks be to God for this comprehensive promise!

What Is the Alternative?

Many religions and philosophies do not endorse the sovereignty of God. Some of their adherents even claim to be *theists* or believers in God. One such philosophy is *open theism*, which, per its name, maintains what its advocates call the *openness of God*. Now, that sounds good, doesn't it? When people are described as *open*, it generally refers to some measure of flexibility. But when open theists describe God as *open*, it is not a good thing. This viewpoint teaches that for God, the future is open to whatever might happen. He doesn't determine what will happen, and, they say, He doesn't even *know* what is going to happen! He is waiting with bated breath like the rest of us to see what's next. One open theist writes that "if God is free and creatures are free, he cannot know in advance always exactly what will happen."[7]

As you can clearly see, to deny the sovereignty of God, open theists must also deny the *omniscience* of God, that God is all-knowing. Denying the sovereignty of God leads to a domino denial of other essential truths about God that are clearly taught in the Scriptures. For example, they might as well deny the power (omnipotence) of

6 Moo, Ibid.

7 Clark Pinnock, "There Is Room for Us: A Reply to Bruce Ware," *JETS* 45 (2002): 216.

God as well. Is God able to intervene when things are going badly for His people? If He doesn't know what's going to happen, does He intervene in what happens, when it happens? Is He even *able* to help? No, open theism pulls the proverbial rug out from our understanding of the nature of God and the certainty of His promises and plan. With regard to the promise that "God causes all things to work together for good" (NASB), how can this possibly be true if God doesn't even *know* how things are going to turn out?

No, since He not only *knows* what is going to come to pass but also *determines* what will happen, all His promises are trustworthy and true. This promise comforts us that nothing takes God by surprise. In fact, His perfect plan is unfolding for our good.

Mark of a Sovereigntist: Faith

Paul writes, "And we *know*." This assurance is a conviction on which we can rely when the storm clouds form in our lives and darkness appears to overwhelm us. We know that God is not wringing His hands in heaven, hoping that things will work out for those who love Him. Though not all things are good in themselves, He has purposed to work all things for good to those who love Him and are called according to His purpose. This is something that we *know*. Notice that Paul doesn't say, "And we *see*." The truth is that we can't always see what God's purpose is in everything that happens to us. As noted earlier and as we will see in some of the upcoming scenarios, we can sometimes discern in hindsight God's purpose in what happens to us. But even when this is the case, we have to admit that our understanding is limited and not comprehensive.

To *know* "that God causes all things to work together for good" (NASB) is therefore *an article of faith, not sight*. An important mark of a sovereigntist is faith. In the eleventh chapter of the book of Hebrews, the writer provides a "hall of faith," a summary of biblical characters who exemplified trust in God through the ages. It includes Noah, Abraham, Moses, Rahab, and David, along with many others. The chapter opens with these profound words: "Now faith is the assurance of things hoped for, the conviction of *things not seen*" (Heb. 11:1, emphasis added). What characterizes faith that is commended by God is trusting Him and His Word even when you cannot *see* the outcome.

This might include suffering. Consider what those in the hall of faith endured: "Some were tortured, refusing to accept release, so that they might rise again to a better life. Others suffered mocking and flogging, and even chains and imprisonment. They were stoned, they were sawn in two, they were killed with the sword. They went about in skins of sheep and goats, destitute, afflicted, mistreated—of whom the world was not worthy—wandering about in deserts and mountains, and in dens and caves of the earth" (vv. 35–38). The writer concludes that they believed even though they did not *receive* what was promised. When you suffer and cannot see the point or the purpose of it, *believe* that God is working out His purpose for your good and His glory.

When you walk by faith and not by sight, it is pleasing to God. In fact, "without faith it is impossible to please him, for whoever would draw near to God must believe that he exists and that he rewards those who seek him" (v. 6).

A Case Study in Faith

The gospel of Matthew records a remarkable exchange between Jesus and a Roman centurion.[8] We don't know the centurion's name, but

8 Read the narrative in Matthew 8:5–13.

we know that he was a gentile with whom Jews were not supposed to interact. We also know that he was an officer in the Roman army. As his title implies, he was the commander of a "century" of soldiers, consisting of a hundred legionnaires. The legionnaires were the very picture of Roman strength and violence. They were the soldiers who conquered, held, and defended imperial territory. Judea was one of the conquered and occupied territories, and Roman soldiers were despised and feared. To say the least, this centurion was one of the toughest of the tough guys. How he had heard about Jesus we do not know, but he came to Him and said, "Lord, my servant is lying paralyzed at home, suffering terribly" (Matt. 8:6). First, it is quite amazing that the centurion himself came to speak to Jesus. He could have sent a servant to find Jesus, but he spoke to Him personally.

Second, the centurion's concern for his servant also seems unusual. Jesus replied that He would come immediately and heal the servant.

Third, the centurion addressed Jesus as "Lord." While this is sometimes translated as "sir," a respectful form of address, most often in Matthew's gospel it is a title of deity. When the centurion addresses Jesus as "Lord" the second time, the intention in the title is clear because the most significant element of the exchange follows. Instead of showing Jesus the way to his sick servant, the centurion replied: "Lord, I am not worthy to have you come under my roof, but only say the word, and my servant will be healed. For I too am a man under authority, with soldiers under me. And I say to one, 'Go,' and he goes, and to another, 'Come,' and he comes, and to my servant, 'Do this,' and he does it" (vv. 8–9).

What was Jesus' response to the centurion? "When Jesus heard this, he marveled and said to those who followed him, 'Truly, I tell you, with no one in Israel have I found such faith'" (v. 10). The verb translated "marveled"[9] is usually reserved for the response of people to the miracles and teaching of Jesus. The only other time in Scripture when Jesus "marveled" at people was when He was in Nazareth and "marveled because of their unbelief" (Mark 6:6). What was it about the centurion that amazed Jesus? What was it that elevated this man above Jesus' own disciples and their fellow Israelites? It was his faith. He knew that Jesus didn't have to be present to heal. He knew that Jesus did not need to lay hands on his servant to heal him. He recognized the power and the authority of Jesus to sovereignly order circumstances so as to bring about His will. Whether he knew it or not, the centurion was a sovereigntist. The narrative concludes with these words: "And to the centurion Jesus said, 'Go; let it be done for you as you have believed.' And the servant was healed at that very moment" (Matt. 8:13).

Therefore, a key characteristic of a sovereigntist is faith. It is believing in the power and the authority of God to accomplish His perfect will *concerning me*. It is believing the promise that "all things work together for good, for those who are called according to his purpose."

For Further Reflection

1. Take a moment to reflect on the fact that God can make and keep His promises to you only because He is sovereign over all things.

9 The Greek verb is *thaumazō*.

2. Can you think of an example in which you can now see, in hindsight, how the Lord used for your good what you considered at the time to be a setback?
3. Can you think of how God has introduced something good into your life for your good?
4. How does faith fit into the life of the sovereigntist? Are you willing to believe that God is at work for your good in your current struggles?

Part Two

SEASONS OF LIFE UNDER GOD'S SOVEREIGN CARE

3

When It's Bright and Sunny

When Things Are Going Well

"Rejoice always, pray without ceasing, give thanks in all circumstances; for this is the will of God in Christ Jesus for you."
(1 Thess. 5:16–18)

You might think that the place to begin our look at the implications of the doctrine of the sovereignty of God is when things go wrong: when tragedy strikes or when things look bleak. But this chapter addresses another matter that might surprise you. It is important to recognize the sovereignty of God in your life not only when things are difficult but also when things are going well. It is so easy for us to forget God when things are going along smoothly.

This very point was addressed by the Lord in the book of Deuteronomy as He prepared His people to enter the promised land. This land had been promised to Abraham generations previously, and the time had now come for them to claim this sacred inheritance. As they anticipated receiving this remarkable gift of God, He declared many promises, but He also issued very clear warnings. He told them to be sure to keep His commandments and not to worship idols. Among the warnings is one against something that is all too human: forgetting God when things go well and taking the credit ourselves. First of all, the Lord reminded the people of the blessings they had received and would receive:

> "And you shall eat and be full, and you shall bless the LORD your God for the good land he has given you.
>
> "Take care lest you forget the LORD your God by not keeping his commandments and his rules and his statutes, which I command you today, lest, when you have eaten and are full and have built good houses and live in them, and when your herds and flocks multiply and your silver and gold is multiplied and all that you have is multiplied . . ." (Deut. 8:10–13)

These words give a perfect picture of how God kept His promises and provided ample food, comfortable houses, healthy flocks, and abundant wealth. What should the result be? It should be gratitude and obedience. But what is the warning? The sentence continues: "then your heart be lifted up, and you forget the LORD your God, who brought you out of the land of Egypt" (v. 14).

Unfortunately, our tendency is to forget the faithfulness of the Lord when things go well. The text goes on to remind the people of everything God had done to bring them to this place of blessedness: "out of the house of slavery, who led you through the great and terrifying wilderness, with its fiery serpents and scorpions and thirsty ground where there was no water, who brought you water out of the flinty rock, who fed you in the wilderness with manna that your fathers did not know, that he might humble you and test you, to do you good in the end" (vv. 14–16). That's right; God had delivered His people through miraculous means from centuries of slavery in Egypt. He had delivered them from the plagues that afflicted their Egyptian oppressors. When the livestock of the Egyptians died, the flocks of God's people had been protected. Remember? A deadly hailstorm had come and destroyed crops and any living thing that failed to take cover, except in the land of Goshen, where the Israelites lived. Remember? When there was darkness all over the land of Egypt, a darkness that could be felt (Ex. 10:21), the Israelites had had light in their homes. Remember? When the firstborn of every family of Egypt and of the livestock were struck down, the families of God's people had been untouched. Remember? God had saved them from venomous snakes in the wilderness. Remember? He had provided drinking water from a rock, twice! Remember? He had fed them bread from heaven. Remember?

Look back on the ways that the Lord has provided for you and has brought you to the circumstances that you enjoy right now, including your comfortable home and your abundant possessions. Remember? Have you forgotten that everything is a blessing from the Lord? I remember that in the early days of our marriage, my wife and I ran out of money before we ran out of month. We had to borrow quarters from our daughter's piggy bank to buy milk for the family. I remember when the cars we drove always broke down right before Christmas or before we went on vacation. Things are much better now. We can now see that all along, the Lord was providing for all our needs.

One of the reasons that we fail to remember God's goodness is that the goodness of God can become "normal." Arthur Pink writes:

> Gratitude is the return justly required from the objects of His beneficence; yet it is often withheld from our great Benefactor *simply because His goodness is so constant and so abundant.* It is lightly esteemed because it is exercised toward us in the common course of events. *It is not felt because we daily experience it.*[1]

Abundant life in the promised land became so "normal" that the people forgot the hardships from which they had been delivered and the blessings that had replaced them: plenty instead of want, security instead of danger, and freedom instead of oppression. So it can be with us. Our everyday blessings become so common that we forget the Source and take them and Him for granted. Here is how Bernard of Clairvaux expressed it: "To see a man humble under prosperity is one of the greatest rarities in the world."[2]

Only one thing is worse than forgetting that the Lord has provided you with every good thing: it is taking credit for it yourself! This is exactly where the text goes next:

> "Beware lest you say in your heart, '*My power and the might of my hand have gotten me this wealth.*' *You shall remember the* L*ORD* *your God, for it is he who gives you power to get wealth,* that he may confirm his covenant that he swore to your fathers, as it is this day. And if you forget the LORD your God and go after other gods and serve them and worship them, I solemnly warn you today that you shall surely perish." (Deut. 8:17–19, emphasis added)

---

1 Arthur W. Pink, *The Attributes of God* (Grand Rapids, Mich.: Baker, 2006), 60 (emphasis added).

2 Quoted in John Flavel, *A Treatise on the Keeping of the Heart* (New York: American Tract Society, 1801), 25.

Our tendency is to blame God when things are bad and then to take the credit when things go well. Sound familiar? Sure, you have made good use of the gifts and talents that the Lord has given to you and have developed a career that has provided the good things that you enjoy now. But don't forget that the Lord has given you "power to get wealth." Every talent and ability has been given to you by our sovereign Lord.

In the book of James, we read, "Every good gift and every perfect gift is from above, coming down from the Father of lights, with whom there is no variation or shadow due to change" (James 1:17). In speaking of spiritual gifts, Paul exhorts: "What do you have that you did not receive? If then you received it, why do you boast as if you did not receive it?" (1 Cor. 4:7). This principle applies to everything that we have: talents, aptitudes, material possessions, and even relationships. Yes, you have developed them, and this is your responsibility. In the same chapter, Paul writes that "it is required of stewards that they be found faithful" (v. 2). The heart of the idea of stewardship is of a trust given to another by the owner. Good gifts have been entrusted to us by God, and we are responsible for taking care of them and developing them. There is never an excuse to say, "My power and the might of my hand have gotten me this wealth" (Deut. 8:17). This leads to arrogance and a superiority complex over others.

Nebuchadnezzar, king of Babylon, was an example of the dangers of such an attitude. In Daniel chapter 4, he was walking on the roof of his royal palace, and he "reflected and said, 'Is this not Babylon the great, which I myself have built as a royal residence by the might of my power and for the glory of my majesty?'" (Dan. 4:30, NASB). The response of the true King was quick in coming:

> While the word was in the king's mouth, a voice came from heaven, saying, "King Nebuchadnezzar, to you it is declared: sovereignty has been removed from you, and you will be driven away from mankind, and your dwelling place will be with the beasts of the field. You will be given grass to eat like cattle, and seven periods of time will pass over you until you recognize that the Most High is ruler over the realm of mankind and bestows it on whomever He wishes." (vv. 31–32, NASB)

The story continues to reveal that exactly what had been predicted came upon Nebuchadnezzar. He was arguably the greatest human sovereign in the world at the time, but he failed to recognize that those who are blessed with power in this world, and everything that goes with it, are indebted to the Great Sovereign. It is rare that pride and arrogance are met with such a swift response, but being humbled is exactly what we deserve when we fail to acknowledge the Lord as the source of every blessing.

Daniel's narrative tells us that Nebuchadnezzar learned his lesson. Here is his own testimony:

> But at the end of that period, I, Nebuchadnezzar, raised my eyes toward heaven and my reason returned to me, and I blessed the Most High and praised and honored Him who lives forever;
>
> > For His dominion is an everlasting dominion,
> > And His kingdom endures from generation to generation.
> > All the inhabitants of the earth are accounted as nothing,
> > But He does according to His will in the host of heaven
> > And among the inhabitants of earth;

> And no one can ward off His hand
> Or say to Him, "What have You done?"
>
> At that time my reason returned to me. And my majesty and splendor were restored to me for the glory of my kingdom, and my counselors and my nobles began seeking me out; so I was reestablished in my sovereignty, and surpassing greatness was added to me. Now I, Nebuchadnezzar, praise, exalt and honor the King of heaven, for all His works are true and His ways just, and He is able to humble those who walk in pride. (Dan. 4:34–37, NASB)

There is no room for boasting in the life of the sovereigntist. We have received everything we have from our gracious God.

Understanding this principle also serves as an antidote for jealousy and envy, doesn't it? When you see others prosper or "doing better" than you are, remember that *they* have only what they have received, too. Though others might not appreciate what they have received or from whom it came, you do. There will always be people who have more money, more talent, and more ability than you. But for you and what you have received, there is no room for boasting; and toward what *others* have received, there is no room for envy or jealousy. Proverbs 14:30 warns that "envy makes the bones rot." You don't need that. Rather, this perspective makes room for you to express your sincere appreciation to others for what God has given *to them*. Belief in God as the sovereign dispenser of gifts and talents frees you from the stress and rotting force of envy and releases you to encourage and value others. Since it is based on genuine appreciation of another person's gifts, aptitudes, and talents, it is not flattery. Flattery is praising another with the ultimate goal of *advancing oneself*—for example, praising the boss regularly with the ultimate goal of getting a promotion. You can easily see that while this tactic is often effective, it is duplicitous. In Proverbs we read, "A man who flatters his neighbor spreads a net for his feet" (Prov. 29:5). Instead of using flattering words for your own advantage, you are freed to express *sincere* appreciation for what God has given to others. We are free to do this enthusiastically when we see that He is the sovereign Giver of every gift.

Mark of a Sovereigntist: Gratitude

In a church I once served, one of our godly elders began every prayer with these words: "Dear Lord, we thank You for *all* things." I italicized *all* because Bob would emphasize *all* and draw it out in his distinctive Southern drawl as if to emphasize the need for our comprehensive thankfulness for the Lord's comprehensive goodness. I'm sure that he was taking his cue from Paul's first letter to the Thessalonians, in which he urged his readers, "Rejoice always, pray without ceasing, *give thanks in all circumstances*; for this is the will of God in Christ Jesus for you" (1 Thess. 5:16–18, emphasis added). One of the first things that we teach our children is to say "please" and "thank you." Saying "thank you" should be a rudimentary instinct of the children of God.

First and foremost, this includes gratitude for forgiveness and for the gift of eternal life through Jesus Christ. Paul reminds us to thank God for "His indescribable gift!" (2 Cor. 9:15, NASB). The word translated "indescribable"[3] is used only here in the New Testament and describes something that "cannot fully be described with

3 Greek *anekdiēgētō*.

human words."[4] Have you ever been given a gift that left you speechless? If you are a Christian, you have! In reminding the Corinthian church about the glorious victory of Jesus over sin and death, Paul says, "Thanks be to God, who gives us the victory through our Lord Jesus Christ" (1 Cor. 15:57). It is Jesus' victory, but He has shared it with us.

There are additional blessings for which we should be thankful every day. Cultivating thankfulness during the good times establishes a rallying point for all times. Jerry Bridges notes: "Thankfulness to God is a recognition that God in His goodness and faithfulness has provided for us and cared for us, both physically and spiritually. It is a recognition that we are totally dependent upon Him; that all that we are and have comes from God."[5]

In conclusion, remember the Lord when things are going well, too! Don't forget to thank Him regularly. In addition to his admonition to give thanks in all circumstances, Paul could also write from prison: "I have learned in whatever situation I am to be content. I know how to be brought low, and I know how to abound. In any and every circumstance, I have learned the secret of facing plenty and hunger, abundance and need. I can do all things through him who strengthens me" (Phil. 4:11–13). Either way, the Lord is sovereign and will give you the strength to be content. The wise author of Ecclesiastes urges, "In the day of prosperity be joyful, and in the day of adversity consider: God has made the one as well as the other" (Eccl. 7:14). C.S. Lewis puts it this way: "We ought to give thanks

---

4 Fritz Rienecker and Cleon Rogers, *Linguistic Key to the Greek New Testament* (Grand Rapids, Mich.: Zondervan, 1980), 484.

5 Jerry Bridges, *The Practice of Godliness* (Carol Stream, Ill.: NavPress, 1996), 100.

for all fortune: if it is good, because it is good, if bad, because it works in us patience, humility and the contempt of this world and the hope of our eternal country."[6]

For Further Reflection

1. Though we often ask "Why?" when things are going poorly, we fail to do so when things are going well. Why are we quick to take credit when things are going well but eager to blame God (or others) when things aren't going our way?
2. How should belief in the sovereignty of God lead to a life of gratitude?
3. How should belief in the sovereignty of God lead to an eagerness to express appreciation for the gifts, talents, and aptitudes of others?
4. Take a few moments now to note and thank God for the many blessings in your life.

6 C.S. Lewis to Don Giovanni Calabria, August 10, 1948, in *The Quotable Lewis*, eds. Wayne Martindale and Jerry Root (Carol Stream, Ill.: Tyndale, 1990), 579.

4

When Storm Clouds Gather

When Things Look Bad

"I believe in a destiny, one I mean, divinely appointed and to which we are carried forward by a perfect trust in God."
—Joshua Chamberlain

One of the most anxious times of life is being in a situation in which you don't know what's going to happen next. It could be anxiety about your health, a relationship, your finances, or any number of other things that you know are on the horizon. We have just seen that the sovereigntist should thank God when things are good and the skies are sunny. But how does it help when you can see something difficult coming down the line? It might happen or it might not. If it does, it will be very bad. From your perspective, it would be better if it did not. Is the light at the end of the tunnel just an oncoming freight train?

Facing Tests of Faith

In order to help with this, I would like you to meet some friends of mine. Their names are Shadrach, Meshach, and Abednego.[1] Actually, their given names were Hananiah, Mishael, and Azariah. They were given their new names by Babylonian officials after they had been taken into captivity there in 586 BC. Nebuchadnezzar was king at the time and built a statue that he declared everyone should bow down to and worship. It was huge! It was ninety feet tall and nine feet wide and was made of pure gold. The signal for the people to fall down and worship was the sound of "horn, pipe, lyre, trigon, harp, bagpipe, and every kind of music" (Dan. 3:5). The consequence for failing to worship this image was quite serious: "And whoever does not fall down and worship shall immediately be cast into a burning fiery furnace" (v. 6). There were to be no excused absences from the required worship. All "peoples, nations, and languages" were to comply (v. 4), which included the Hebrew captives.

The day of the dedication came, and the instruments played, but not everyone paid homage to the grand idol. Shadrach, Meshach, and Abednego did not do so because they were worshipers of the God of their fathers, Abraham, Isaac, and Jacob. They knew that only the true God was to be worshiped. But their failure to comply with Nebuchadnezzar's command was noticed and was not overlooked. Certain individuals "tattled" on the men. More specifically, the text tells us that they "maliciously accused" them (v. 8). Here's what they said: "These men, O king, pay no attention to you; they do not serve your gods or worship the golden image that you have set up" (v. 12). There's one thing that a totalitarian ruler cannot tolerate, and that is to be ignored.

1 Read the whole account in Daniel 3.

The king was furious! He called for the men to give an account for themselves. He asked them whether this was true. But before they had an opportunity to answer, he offered them another chance the next time that the signal came to worship the idol. He also reiterated the fiery fate if they failed to comply. He followed his threat with this question: "And who is the god who will deliver you out of my hands?" (v. 15). The answer to that question would be coming very soon.

Here are three men who were on the precipice of a painful death, knowing what might happen to them if they didn't comply. What was their attitude? What was their response? Did they panic? Here is what they said: "Shadrach, Meshach, and Abednego answered and said to the king, 'O Nebuchadnezzar, we have no need to answer you in this matter. If this be so, our God whom we serve is able to deliver us from the burning fiery furnace, and he will deliver us out of your hand, O king" (vv. 16–17).

The three men didn't need time to think it over. They knew that they were not going to compromise their convictions and bow down to the idol. In answer to the king's challenge, they knew that the Lord was able to save them from death. Of course, He was *able* to do so—but would He? This is the conflict that rises in the hearts of many when they anticipate difficulties. They know that God *is able* to deliver them, but *will* He do so? It was not enough for Shadrach, Meshach, and Abednego to believe and even pray that the Lord would save them. They went a step further: "*But if not*, be it known to you, O king, that we will not serve your gods or worship the golden image that you have set up" (v. 18, emphasis added). They trusted the Lord even if things didn't turn out the way that they might like. They understood that it was God's prerogative to save them or not to save them because He is God. Either way, they were going to trust Him. Sometimes we think that something terrible *cannot* happen or *must not* happen to me or to a loved one. A sovereigntist is willing to say, "But even if it does, I will trust Him."

These men didn't get another opportunity to fail to bow down to the idol because their reply really made the king angry. The narrative says that he "was filled with fury, and the expression of his face was changed" (v. 19). He decided to toss them right into the fiery furnace. In fact, he had the furnace heated seven times hotter. It was so hot that the brave men who threw Shadrach, Meshach, and Abednego into the fiery furnace burned to death. What happened next? "Then King Nebuchadnezzar was astonished and rose up in haste. He declared to his counselors, 'Did we not cast three men bound into the fire?' They answered and said to the king, 'True, O king.' He answered and said, 'But I see four men unbound, walking in the midst of the fire, and they are not hurt; and the appearance of the fourth is like a son of the gods'" (vv. 24–25). Yes, the Lord delivered the three men from this terrible fate. In fact, when they emerged from the furnace, their hair was not singed, nor did their clothes even smell like smoke! The result was that Nebuchadnezzar acknowledged that their God was truly God.

What about the fourth man seen walking around in the furnace with them? He did not emerge with them. Who was he? The narrative tells us that "the appearance of the fourth is like a son of the gods" (v. 25). This was undoubtedly a preincarnate appearance of the Son of God, Jesus Christ.[2] He was the One in the midst of the

---

2 There are several preincarnate appearances of the Son of God in the Old Testament, including Genesis 16:7–10 and Judges 6:11–14.

flames with them and the One who kept them from harm. If God calls you to endure fiery trials, remember that you are not alone. He is with you.

Fast-forward to a garden where you see a man kneeling in prayer. It is the same Jesus Christ, who was anticipating the worst suffering imaginable: death by crucifixion. Yes, others had endured this form of execution, but in addition to its normal torture, His suffering on the cross included bearing the weight of punishment due to our sins. This included the prospect of being "forsaken" by the Father as He atoned for our transgressions (Matt. 27:46). What was Jesus' perspective as He anticipated this suffering? Yes, He asked, "If it be possible, let this cup pass from me" (26:39). He asked three times. He knew that His Father could deliver Him, but He also prayed, "Not as I will, but as you will" (v. 39). It is because of His willingness to suffer that the suffering of this life for us is not final. As we have also seen, when we are called to suffer, it is according to His plan, for His purpose, and for His glory. What are we to learn as sovereigntists? How are we to face difficulties that *might* happen?

Remember That God Is Able to Deliver You, and Pray to That End

Though we have no record of Shadrach, Meshach, and Abednego's praying for deliverance, we can surmise that they did. Earlier in the same book, Daniel had called on these men to pray for wisdom that God would reveal to him not only the interpretation of King Nebuchadnezzar's dream but *the dream itself*. Undoubtedly, these were men of prayer, and they certainly prayed. Jesus asked, "*If it be possible*, let this cup pass from me" (Matt. 26:39, emphasis added). So the first principle is that it is appropriate to pray for healing and a good outcome.

The Scriptures direct us to trust God in prayer rather than worry. Faith also allows us to move forward without being crippled by anxiety. We don't have any insight into the mental state of the Hebrew captives, but in Scripture we are told: "Do not be anxious about anything, but in everything by prayer and supplication with thanksgiving let your requests be made known to God. And the peace of God, which surpasses all understanding, will guard your hearts and your minds in Christ Jesus" (Phil. 4:6–7). This is an amazing imperative because the first human impulse when trouble comes is to worry. Paul tells us to worry about nothing and pray about everything![3]

If we believe that God is sovereign and is working out His plan, we do not need to worry about how things are going to work out. This is not Alfred E. Neuman's "What, me worry?" or Bobby McFerrin's "Don't Worry, Be Happy." It is trusting God for the outcome. In fact, Paul tells us that if we pray instead of worrying, we will have peace. Notice that this doesn't promise that the problems will go away, but teaches us that even in the midst of our problems, anxiety can be replaced by peace.

This peace has a couple of interesting characteristics. First, it is *incomprehensible*. Paul writes that it "surpasses all understanding." This means that it can't be explained from a merely human perspective. Second, the peace that the Lord gives provides *protection*. Paul writes that the Lord's peace "will guard your hearts and your minds." As he wrote these words, Paul was in a Roman prison and could look right at the soldier charged to keep him in protective custody. As Martyn Lloyd-Jones suggests: "It conjures up a picture. What will

---

3 In chapter 9, we will take a look at how God's sovereignty and prayer complement each other.

happen is that this peace of God will walk round the ramparts and towers of our life. We are inside, and the activities of the heart and mind are producing those stresses and anxieties and strains from the outside. But the peace of God will keep them all out and we ourselves inside will be at perfect peace."[4] It is in times of difficulty that we need God's protection over our hearts and minds. The enemy of our souls is all too eager to whisper into our ears that "the Lord can't love you if He allowed this to happen to you," and other such lies. The Lord's peace guards us against the bitterness and cynicism that can blow us off course if we are not anchored in His loving promise of peace. "The name of the Lord is a strong tower; the righteous man runs into it and is safe" (Prov. 18:10).

Remember That Healing and Deliverance Might Not Come

Second, in faith, identify with Shadrach, Meshach, and Abednego, who were ready to trust God with the alternative of His deliverance when they said, "But if not . . ."

In the spring of 2000, Dr. James Montgomery Boice, faithful minister of Tenth Presbyterian Church in Philadelphia for decades, was diagnosed with liver cancer. When addressing his congregation about the diagnosis, he said:

> A relevant question, I guess, when you pray is, pray for what? Should you pray for a miracle? Well, you're free to do that, of course. My general impression is that the God who is able to do miracles—and he certainly can—is also able to keep you from getting the problem

---

4 D. Martyn Lloyd-Jones, *The Life of Peace: An Exposition of Philippians 3 and 4* (Grand Rapids, Mich.: Baker, 1992), 175.

> in the first place. So although miracles do happen, they're rare by definition. A miracle has to be an unusual thing.
>
> I think it's far more profitable to pray for wisdom for the doctors.[5]

He wasn't being a stoic but was looking ahead with Christlike faith, as we see in the following words:

> If I were to reflect on what goes on theologically here, there are two things I would stress. One is the sovereignty of God. That's not novel. We have talked about the sovereignty of God here forever. God is in charge. When things like this come into our lives, they are not accidental. It's not as if God somehow forgot what was going on, and something bad slipped by.

You might wonder what the second "thing" might be. After acknowledging the sovereignty of God, there is still the question whether God cares. Have you wondered about this in the midst of your suffering? Dr. Boice continued:

> God is not only the one who is in charge; God is also good. Everything he does is good. And what Romans 12, verses 1 and 2, says is that we have the opportunity by the renewal of our minds—that is, how we think about these things—actually to prove what God's will

---

5 Quotations from Dr. Boice's statement can be found here: David Burnette, "Should You Pray for a Miracle? Dr. James Boice on God's Sovereign Goodness in Suffering," *The Log College* (blog), June 15, 2015, https://thelogcollege.wordpress.com/2015/06/15/should-you-pray-for-a-miracle-by-james-montgomery-boice/.

> is. And then it says, "His good, pleasing, and perfect will." Is that good, pleasing, and perfect to God? Yes, of course, but the point of it is that it's good, pleasing, and perfect to us. If God does something in your life, would you change it? If you'd change it, you'd make it worse. It wouldn't be as good. So that's the way we want to accept it and move forward, and who knows what God will do?

Dr. Boice passed into glory in June 2000.

Continue to Trust God Moving Forward

What was the evidence of the trust of Shadrach, Meshach, and Abednego? They refused to compromise what they knew to be true. Remember what they said? "But if not, be it known to you, O king, that we will not serve your gods or worship the golden image that you have set up" (Dan. 3:18). Our third principle is that in trying times, we must not give in to the temptation to compromise our convictions. We are to stand firm!

Ultimately, in the case of Shadrach, Meshach, and Abednego, God didn't deliver them *from* the fiery furnace, but He did deliver them *through* it. It could also be said of Dr. Boice that though he wasn't delivered *from* the cancer, he was delivered *through* it to his heavenly home. This is the truth for anything and everything that we face in this life, including that which will one day take us from this life. Ultimately, we will be taken through that last crisis to glory.

This perspective can be ours only because Jesus was delivered through His painful atoning sacrifice to His glorious resurrection and ascension to the right hand of the Father, where He ever lives to intercede for us. This is also the final answer to Nebuchadnezzar's question, "And who is the god who will deliver you out of my hands?" (Dan. 3:15). In God's perfect will, we may be called to suffer at the hands of a human adversary, a terminal disease, or an unforeseen trauma, but for the believer, in every case, Jesus promises: "I give them eternal life, and they will never perish, and no one will snatch them out of my hand. My Father, who has given them to me, is greater than all, and no one is able to snatch them out of the Father's hand" (John 10:28–29).

This assurance enables us to face the future with a faith-filled fearlessness that can proclaim with the Apostle Paul, "I am sure that neither death nor life, nor angels nor rulers, nor things present nor things to come, nor powers, nor height nor depth, nor anything else in all creation, will be able to separate us from the love of God in Christ Jesus our Lord" (Rom. 8:38–39).

Characteristic of a Sovereigntist: Courage

When you are convinced that, whatever comes, God is working out His plan, you can have the kind of faith-filled fearlessness that we saw in the lives of Shadrach, Meshach, and Abednego. There are countless examples of the courage that results when we are convinced that God guides our lives, but I would like to look at a hero of the Civil War: Joshua Lawrence Chamberlain.

As the War between the States was dragging into its third year, General Robert E. Lee determined to invade the North to force the Union to sue for peace. As he crossed through Maryland and into Pennsylvania, a series of troop movements led to a small skirmish that grew into the three-day Battle of Gettysburg from July 1 to 3, 1863. After a bloody first day with no decisive resolution, General Lee decided to test the left flank of the Union line. Anchored at the end of the line on a hill called Little Round Top, Colonel Joshua

Chamberlain and his 20th Maine Regiment were positioned. They were ordered to hold their position at all costs, lest the whole Union Army be outflanked and assaulted from the rear. Several uphill attacks were made by regiments from Texas and Alabama under General John B. Hood's command, but to no avail. Assault after assault was made, draining both sides of men and ammunition. When Colonel Chamberlain recognized that his men were nearly out of bullets, he ordered a bayonet charge down the hill, which stunned the Confederate soldiers and won the day for the Union. The flank held, and the Army of the Potomac survived to win the battle the next day and eventually to win the war.

Chamberlain's leadership has recently been popularized by Michael Sharra's book *The Killer Angels* and the movie *Gettysburg*. But neither of these does justice to the background of Chamberlain, particularly his religious upbringing. He had been raised in a Christian home by devout parents who were part of a church from the rich New England Congregationalist tradition. At the height of his youthful church participation, Chamberlain memorized the Westminster Shorter Catechism from beginning to end. His commitment to memorization of the Bible, the catechism, and poetry would become a signature practice of his adulthood. It undergirded his disciplined character. Although this practice might appear to be strictly a mental exercise, Ronald White, a Chamberlain biographer, described this learning as "by heart."[6]

White was asked how this religious upbringing intersected with Chamberlain's courageous action on Little Round Top. White

6 Ronald C. White, *On Great Fields: The Life and Unlikely Heroism of Joshua Lawrence Chamberlain* (New York: Random House, 2023), 10.

replied, "He was deeply influenced by his faith, his Congregational and Presbyterian upbringing, which led him to have a strong belief in Providence, that God was guiding him and sustaining him, even in the midst of battle."[7]

As the Civil War raged on, Chamberlain led troops in twenty battles, and during the siege of Petersburg in 1864, he was wounded by a bullet that entered his right hip and groin and lodged. Chamberlain was informed that the wound was mortal. His courage to face death through faith in his sovereign God and Savior is evident in these words that he wrote to his dear wife, Fanny:

> My darling wife, I am lying mortally wounded the doctors think, but my mind & heart are at peace. Jesus Christ is my all-sufficient savior. I go to him. God Bless & keep & comfort you, precious one, you have been a precious wife to me. To know & love you makes life & death beautiful. Cherish the darlings & give my love to all the dear ones. Do not grieve too much for me. We shall all soon meet.[8]

In God's providence, Chamberlain would survive his wounds, but it would take a long time for him to recover. While he was convalescing, many thought that he had done enough in his role as a soldier, including his dear mother. But he was determined to rejoin the troops in Petersburg. He wrote to his mother, "I confess, not a selfish ambition: for I assure you not all honors and titles that be

---

7 Ronald White, Comments at the Union League of Philadelphia Library Hour, November 1, 2023.

8 White, *On Great Fields*, 203.

given or won, would tempt me to hazard the happiness and welfare of my dear ones at home, nor would they be an equivalent whatever for these terrible wounds as must cast a shadow over the remainder of my days, even though I should apparently recover." He continued, "I believe in a destiny—one, I mean, divinely appointed, & to which we are carried forward by a perfect trust in God."[9] His biographer comments: "At critical moments in his life, we hear Chamberlain express his faith in a purposeful God. He was not referring to a nineteenth-century fatalism—whatever will be will be—but rather to a Calvinist conviction about a God who acts in history."[10]

Chamberlain's parents had named their firstborn Joshua after the biblical character of the same name because "he left nothing undone of all that the LORD had commanded" (Josh. 11:15). The biblical general Joshua was also a man of great courage, called on by God to bring the Israelite nation from the wilderness in which the people had wandered for forty years to the land that God had promised to his forefathers. In the opening verses of the book that bears his name, God calls on Joshua three times to be "strong and courageous" (1:6, 7, 9). But that call to be courageous is not spoken in a vacuum. The Lord promised Joshua that "the LORD your God is with you wherever you go" (v. 9). This is the same promise that God makes to you: "I will never leave you nor forsake you" (Heb. 13:5). When the waves of trouble rise around you, never doubt that the Lord is with you.

Courage is also the fruit of obedience to God's Word. Along with the promises to Joshua came this command: "This Book of the

---

9 White, 208.

10 White, Comments, November 1, 2023. After the war, Chamberlain would be elected governor of Maine four times and then become the president of his alma mater, Bowdoin College. He died in 1914 at the ripe old age of eighty-five.

Law shall not depart from your mouth, but you shall meditate on it day and night, so that you may be careful to do according to all that is written in it. For then you will make your way prosperous, and then you will have good success" (Josh. 1:8). The courage of our convictions and commitments enables us to stand strong when facing life's obstacles.

As we conclude this chapter, we must include one more courageous Joshua. We know Him as Jesus, but His Hebrew name was Jeshua or Joshua. You recall that the angel told Joseph, His stepfather, that Jeshua was to be His name, "for he will save his people from their sins" (Matt. 1:21). This was the most remarkable mission of all. Don't you think it odd that you rarely hear about the *courage* of Jesus? Have you ever heard a sermon or read an article about His courage? Can't *courage* be defined as moving forward in spite of the scope of the mission or the power of an adversary? Was there ever a mission more consequential than being the Savior of the world? Were there ever adversaries more powerful than death and Satan himself? Much of the mission of Jesus we cannot understand, but we do know that it included bearing the penalty for our sins and overcoming death itself. It was so daunting that Jesus Himself prayed three times, "My Father, if it be possible, let this cup pass from me" (26:39)—"this cup" being the suffering that He was about to endure. But you will remember that courage finds its anchor in obedience, and Jesus said, "Nevertheless, not as I will, but as you will" (v. 39).

Not before or since has there been anyone else who perfectly kept God's law, but Jesus did. He courageously accomplished His mission. By faith, we share in His victory and, through His Spirit, know His courage. Paul exults:

> What then shall we say to these things? If God is for us, who can be against us? He who did not spare his own Son but gave him up for us all, how will he not also with him graciously give us all things? Who shall bring any charge against God's elect? It is God who justifies. Who is to condemn? Christ Jesus is the one who died—more than that, who was raised—who is at the right hand of God, who indeed is interceding for us. Who shall separate us from the love of Christ? Shall tribulation, or distress, or persecution, or famine, or nakedness, or danger, or sword? (Rom. 8:31–35)

The answer is, of course, that no one and nothing can separate you from the love of Christ. When the storm clouds form, don't cower but have courage. When the floodwaters rise, don't flee but trust Him for the courage to stand firm.

For Further Reflection

1. What is your first reaction when it looks like something bad is about to happen?
2. Do you believe that God is able to deliver you? Are you asking Him to do so?
3. Are you willing to say with Shadrach, Meshach, and Abednego, "But if not"—that is, if the Lord does not deliver you, or if things don't work out the way you think they should, you will trust Him?
4. How does trust in the plan of God produce courage in your life right now?

5

In the Middle of the Storm

When Things Go Terribly Wrong

"We do not know what to do, but our eyes are on you."
(2 Chron. 20:12)

Sometimes life delivers a blow that is severe and unexpected. There is a shocking death or a stunning diagnosis. How can these things be part of God's plan? How can we see that these things are working together for good (see Rom. 8:28)? How can this be so in the worst of times? If God is sovereign, why does He allow these things to happen to us?

I have a friend with whom I attended seminary and who upon graduation became the minister of outreach at Coral Ridge Presbyterian Church in Fort Lauderdale, Fla. While serving there, he made several close friends, including Jack Mowday. Jack's wife, Lois, once wanted to surprise her husband with a unique Christmas present. He had always wanted to go on a hot-air balloon ride, and she was determined to make it happen, but it was very expensive. Lois asked my friend whether he would be willing to go along and share the surprise and the cost. After consulting with his wife, my friend concluded that the adventure was a little too expensive for them, so with regrets, he declined the invitation.

A few days before Christmas that year, the surprise was sprung, to Jack's delight, and he and two of his friends set out along with the pilot. Sadly, the wicker gondola struck four power lines and turned into a fireball. The pilot was unable to land the balloon, and the heat from the fire caused the balloon to rise. With their families watching in horror as they followed by car, two of the passengers jumped from the flaming basket, one at 150 feet and the other at 1,500 feet. All occupants of the gondola fell to their deaths. It is difficult to imagine the heartbreak of the wives and children as they rushed to the lifeless bodies of their loved ones.

Where did they find their comfort? First, they found comfort in the fact that they knew that their loved ones were in heaven. First responders reported being amazed as they came on the scene, listening to the tearful women comforting their children with the assurance that their loved ones were in heaven. Those dads and husbands were men of faith, and they knew that for the believer in Jesus, to be absent from the body is to be present with the Lord (2 Cor. 5:8). Of course, the families were devastated, but there was comfort in the knowledge that their husbands and dads were safely "home" with the Lord.

The second source of comfort speaks directly to the peace that the sovereigntist experiences during such times. My pastor friend and his wife visited Lois shortly after the accident. As they shed tears together, Lois turned and said, "I would have gone crazy had I not believed in the sovereignty of God." What did she mean by this? From a human perspective, she had arranged for the balloon ride. She had made all the arrangements, not only for Jack but for his friends. She had chosen the day. Carrying this logic to its conclusion, she could have concluded that she was responsible for her husband's death. But she was a woman of faith and understood that behind these events was the mystery of God's plan and providence. In this truth she found peace and comfort.

The answer to the "Why [with a capital *W*] did this happen?" question is hidden in the counsel of God's will. Sometimes, however, there are answers to "Why [with a lowercase *w*] did this happen?" In the case of the death of Jack Mowday and his friends, the faith-filled testimonies of the family members led many to saving faith in Jesus Christ and others to enter full-time Christian ministry. But the answer to the "Why?" question is left to the mystery of God's divine purposes.

Remember, however, the promise of God: "And we know that God causes all things to work together for good to those who love God, to those who are called according to His purpose" (Rom. 8:28, NASB). As we observed in chapter 2 in commenting on this promise, the verse does not say that "all things are good"—because not all things are good. Death is not good. It is described as our "enemy" (1 Cor. 15:26). In fact, a friend whose fourteen-year-old daughter died suddenly came up with an accurate expression to describe death and its aftermath. She simply said, "This stinks." She is exactly right! Many of the things we experience are terrible. But this is not the end of the story for those who trust in the Lord. Romans 8:28 teaches that all things "*work together* for good." As Jerry Bridges has observed: "God will never allow any action against you that is not in accord with His will for you. And His will is always directed to our good."[1] Yes, we grieve, but we grieve embracing the promise of life

---

1 Jerry Bridges, *Trusting God* (Carol Stream, Ill.: NavPress, 1988), 71.

after death based on the resurrection of Jesus from the dead! When we are in the middle of difficulties, there are certain traps to avoid.

Traps to Avoid

Trap One: Selective Memory

When we are in the middle of such challenges, we are tempted to idealize the past. When we are walking in the dark valley, we might long for the sunny slopes of former days. In the midst of Job's suffering, he lamented, "Oh, that I were as in the months of old, as in the days when God watched over me, when his lamp shone upon my head, and by his light I walked through darkness, as I was in my prime" (Job 29:2–4). What does the wise writer of Ecclesiastes have to say about this trap? "Say not, 'Why were the former days better than these?' For it is not from wisdom that you ask this" (Eccl. 7:10).

Idealizing the past is not wise; things in the past were probably *not* as good as you remember. Looking longingly backward was one of the stumbling blocks of the Israelites in the wilderness when they became tired of eating manna day in and day out: "Now the rabble that was among them had a strong craving. And the people of Israel also wept again and said, 'Oh that we had meat to eat! We remember the fish we ate in Egypt that cost nothing, the cucumbers, the melons, the leeks, the onions, and the garlic. But now our strength is dried up, and there is nothing at all but this manna to look at'" (Num. 11:4–6). But *what did they forget* about the "former days"? They forgot that they had been slaves in Egypt. They forgot that Pharaoh had ordered the death of all male Hebrew babies. They forgot the deliverance from bondage from one of the greatest earthly powers through a multitude of miracles. *What did they remember* about the "former days"?

They remembered meat, fish, cucumbers, melons, leeks, onions, and garlic! This is selective memory, indeed! Sadly, it demonstrated a lack of gratitude that led to a bitterness against the Lord that He had to address.

Don't you think that we can be guilty of idealizing the good old days? Our minds in retrospect are prone to highlight the good things and suppress the difficulties we faced. Sure, there may have been days when you had more money, or a better job, or better relationships. From time to time, I have pondered whether I would like to be eighteen years old again. After some thought, my answer has been, "No, because I would not want to relive all the challenging times again!"

Trap Two: Overlooking Current Blessings

The second trap is related to the first in that idealizing the past often leads to lack of contentment and appreciation for what the Lord is providing *now*. Granted, the Israelites in the wilderness ate the same thing every day for forty years. After all, there were only so many ways that manna could be prepared. But while the people remembered what they used to eat in Egypt, they failed to appreciate the fact that in the desert, in the middle of nowhere, they had something to eat *every day*! Every single morning it was there. There was even a double portion on the sixth morning of the week so that they would not have to go out and gather food on the Sabbath. Instead of complaining, they should have reflected on the fact that the Lord provided for their needs every day.

What about you? Though you might think fondly of past times, are you neglecting the goodness of God to you *right now*? Have you failed to be grateful for what He provides for you every day?

One of the saddest books in the Bible is Lamentations. It was written by Jeremiah in the wake of the destruction of Jerusalem by the Babylonians in 586 BC. The book is mostly gloom and doom, but right in the middle of the book are these words of hope:

> The steadfast love of the LORD never ceases;
> his mercies never come to an end;
> they are new every morning;
> great is your faithfulness.
> "The LORD is my portion," says my soul,
> "therefore I will hope in him." (Lam. 3:22–24)

Jerusalem had been destroyed and its population carried away into captivity. Worst of all, the temple had been demolished and burned and its treasures hauled away. Yet in the midst of all this, Jeremiah reminds us that there is always hope. Every morning there is hope. Why? Because God is always faithful and His love for His people never changes. You can also be sure that in Jesus, God loves you every single day and that therefore there is always hope. Even as manna came to His people every day in the wilderness, you can be sure that He is with you every morning. On that foundation, you can then reflect on the other "mercies" that He has provided for you: daily bread, forgiveness, and the Holy Spirit, too!

Trap Three: Doubting God's Goodness

In *The Problem of Pain*, C.S. Lewis identifies a third way of thinking to which we might yield when things go wrong: "If God were good, He would wish to make His creatures perfectly happy, and if God were almighty He would be able to do what He wished. But the creatures are not happy. Therefore God lacks either goodness, or power, or both."[2]

But let's consider the possibility that "our happiness" is not the ultimate goal of our Creator. What if there is a higher goal in mind? That is difficult for us to imagine, since we have been so inundated with "it's all about you" marketing. Lewis challenges this mindset and this view of God: "What would really satisfy us would be a God who said of anything we happened to like doing, 'What does it matter so long as they are contented?' We want, in fact, not so much a Father in Heaven as a grandfather in heaven—a senile benevolence who, as they say, 'liked to see young people enjoying themselves' and whose plan for the universe was simply that it might be truly said at the end of each day, 'a good time was had by all.'"[3] What Lewis is getting at is that when we love someone, we want to see him grow and we want to see him improve. What this requires does not always make the person happy. Among the clearest examples of this are the restrictions and discipline we exercise to help bring our children to maturity. Do they like doing their part around the house? No. Do they like sharing with their siblings? Not a chance. Do they like treating adults respectfully? No way! While they are learning these lessons, are they happy? Nope.

God's love has an even greater goal in mind. It is not to make us happy but to conform us to the image of His Son (Rom. 8:29). *That* is quite an undertaking! To transform selfish sinners into people who treat others the way that they would like to be treated isn't easy.[4] To develop people who love others as Christ sacrificially loved

---

2 C.S. Lewis, *The Problem of Pain* (1940; repr., New York: HarperOne, 1996), 16.

3 Lewis, *Problem of Pain*, 31.

4 The Golden Rule: "So whatever you wish that others would do to you, do also to them, for this is the Law and the Prophets" (Matt. 7:12).

them[5]—that is a tall order. But this is God's objective for His people. Lewis writes, "We are, not metaphorically but in very truth, a Divine work of art, something that God is making, and therefore something with which He will not be satisfied until it has a certain character."[6] His craft includes shaping and molding. It includes "knocking the rough edges off."

Sometimes this includes enduring hardship of many kinds. Like little children, we resist the process, but the Lord knows the end He has in mind for us. Lewis rightly observes that "it is natural for us to wish that God had designed for us a less glorious and less arduous destiny; but then we are wishing not for more love but for less."[7] He loved you so much that He sent His Son into the world to save you from the penalty of sin by believing in Him.[8] But that's not all. He is determined to save you from the weighty power of sin,[9] and you will eventually be saved from the very presence of sin when you are perfectly conformed to the image of Jesus.[10] It's the fight against the impulses of sin that requires the convergence of His powerful Spirit and our yielded wills.

Lewis again notes, "We may wish, indeed, that we were of so little account to God that He left us alone to follow our natural impulses—that He would give over trying to train us into something so unlike our natural selves: but once again, we are asking not for

---

5 The Platinum Rule: "A new commandment I give to you, that you love one another: just as I have loved you, you also are to love one another" (John 13:34).

6 Lewis, *Problem of Pain*, 34.

7 Lewis, *Problem of Pain*, 35.

8 This is the gracious act of *justification* by faith.

9 This is the process of *sanctification*.

10 This is the act of *glorification*.

more Love, but for less."[11] Have you ever thought of God's showing His love to you through trials this way?

Someone once said, "God might take us the way we are, but He won't leave us that way." Here is another important promise, from the pen of Paul: "I am sure of this, that he who began a good work in you will bring it to completion at the day of Jesus Christ" (Phil. 1:6). We are not like neglected household projects that are half-completed and unlikely to be attended to. What God starts, He finishes. We must acknowledge that some of His loving "renovations" will include hardship and pain. In the midst of his trials, Job declared to one of his comforters, "He knows the way that I take; when he has tried me, I shall come out as gold" (Job 23:10).

When we are in the middle of the storm, not only are there traps to avoid, but there are positive steps we can take.

What to Do in the Midst of the Terrible Storm

Keep Your Eyes on Him: Trust in the Lord

The first thing that we need to do is to make sure that we are keeping our eyes focused on the Lord instead of on our circumstances. A biblical story that comes to mind is the occasion that Jesus sent His disciples ahead to cross the Sea of Galilee while He remained behind to pray.[12] He decided to catch up with them, but it seemed that no other boats were available at that time of night,[13] so He decided to walk—on the water! As He approached the boat, the disciples saw

---

11 Lewis, *Problem of Pain*, 36.

12 Read the whole account in Matthew 14:22–33.

13 The text says that this occurred during the fourth watch of the night, which was between 3 and 6 a.m.

Him, and of course they were terrified. Wouldn't you be? When Peter saw Jesus walking on the water, he asked Jesus whether he could take a walk on the water, too. Jesus urged him to come. Peter stepped out of the boat, and what do you know—he, too, was walking on the water! But it was one of those moments in life when Peter must have asked himself, "What have I just done?" Here is how Matthew describes what happened next: "But when he saw the wind, he was afraid, and beginning to sink he cried out, 'Lord, save me'" (Matt. 14:30). It is so interesting that it was "when he *saw the wind*" that Peter was afraid. You would have thought that it would be seeing the waves, but it was the wind and likely the wind's effect on the waves. But the wind was at the forefront of Peter's fear. He began to sink.

Peter was in a serious situation,[14] and he knew it. When he called for help, Jesus reached out and took his hand and brought him safely into the boat. It is fair to say that Peter's problem was looking at the wind and the waves instead of at Jesus. As Jesus brought him back onboard, He said, "O you of little faith, why did you doubt?" (Matt. 14:31). Isn't this our problem in the midst of the storm? Don't we tend to look at the problems, the pain, and the loss instead of at the Lord? The result is that sinking feeling of helplessness. The answer? Look to Jesus, "the founder and perfecter of our faith, who for the joy that was set before him endured the cross, despising the shame, and is seated at the right hand of the throne of God" (Heb. 12:2).

For Peter on the sea, the intervention of Jesus meant instant relief. In fact, Matthew reports that as soon as Jesus and Peter stepped into the boat, "the wind ceased" (Matt. 14:32). Peter's crisis was brief and

---

14 In the only other occurrence in the New Testament of the word translated "sink" in Matthew 14:30, it implies drowning (see Matt. 18:6).

was brought to a swift resolution when he cried out to Jesus. Many of our crises are not short-lived but lifelong. You might be surrounded by the wind and the waves right now, but the solution is the same: look to Jesus and not at the wind and waves; trust in Him and His good plan.

Consider also a historical figure. Dietrich Bonhoeffer was a sovereigntist who lived and died in Germany during the darkest days of the twentieth century. He was academically brilliant and was criticized by family members when he decided to pursue theology. He became a Lutheran pastor, a theologian, and part of the Confessing Church movement that set itself against the rise of Adolf Hitler and his Nazi Party. Bonhoeffer was also part of the resistance to the ongoing treachery of the Third Reich. In fact, he was part of the conspiracy that led to the failed Stauffenberg attempt on Hitler's life in July 1944. He was eventually identified as a coconspirator and was imprisoned at Flossenbürg concentration camp, where he was executed early on the morning of April 9, 1945. The Allies liberated Flossenbürg two weeks later.

Early in his ministry, as the shadow of National Socialism was falling over Germany, Bonhoeffer preached a sermon at the *Dreifaltigkeitskirche* (Holy Trinity Church) in Berlin. The text for the sermon was 2 Chronicles 20:12: "We do not know what to do, but our eyes are on you."[15] They were the words of the prayer of King Jehoshaphat of Judah when hostile nations rose up against him. The king's comfort was not in looking at the danger around him but in looking at the Lord above. The Lord assured the king with these words: "Do not be afraid and do not be dismayed at this great horde, for the battle is not yours but God's" (v. 15).

15 Read the entire narrative in 2 Chronicles 20.

The next morning, Jehoshaphat commanded a most unusual army, which was led by those appointed "to sing to the LORD and praise him in holy attire, as they went before the army" (v. 21). As they advanced, they sang, "Give thanks to the LORD, for his steadfast love endures forever" (v. 21). The text goes on to say that when the singing began, the Lord "set an ambush" for Israel's enemies (v. 22), causing them to fight against one another and destroy one another.

For the Israelites, looking to the Lord resulted in deliverance from their earthly enemies. For Bonhoeffer, it led to a different kind of deliverance, from death to life. He viewed death as a station on the road to freedom:

> No one has yet believed in God and the kingdom of God, no one has yet heard about the realm of the resurrected, and not been homesick from that hour, waiting and looking forward joyfully to being released from bodily existence. Why are we so afraid when we think about death? Death is only dreadful for those who live in dread and fear of it. Death is not wild and terrible, if only we can be still and hold fast to God's Word.
>
> How do we know that dying is so dreadful? Who knows whether, in our human fear and anguish we are only shivering and shuddering at the most glorious, heavenly, blessed event in the world?
>
> Death is hell and night and cold, if it is not transformed by our faith. But that is just what is so marvelous, that we can transform death.[16]

---

16 Excerpt from Bonhoeffer's "Stations on the Road to Freedom," in Eric Metaxas, *Bonhoeffer: Pastor, Martyr, Prophet, Spy* (Nashville, Tenn.: Thomas Nelson, 2010), 531.

Such was the sentiment of young Bonhoeffer as his beloved country was hurtling toward war and atrocities that the world had not known until that time. This was also the text that Franz Hildebrandt preached at Bonhoeffer's memorial service on July 27, 1945. Hildebrandt was a Confessing Church pastor and friend of Bonhoeffer who had also been imprisoned but survived the war.

Many times when things go wrong, we "do not know what to do," but remember that the sovereigntist expands the perspective from the strictly horizontal level of the pain to include the vertical trust in the Lord. When you don't know what to do, keep your eyes on Him.

Ask for God's Help

I have met people over the course of my ministry who have thought that it is "unspiritual" to pray for themselves. Yet this view is quite contrary to the teaching of the Bible. In fact, in the Lord's Prayer, Jesus instructs His disciples to pray for their daily bread, forgiveness of sins, relief from temptation, and deliverance from the evil one (see Matt. 6:9–13).

Over and over again in Scripture, we read about God's people crying out to Him for relief. In the book of Psalms, we see examples of these heartfelt cries for help. Here are a few examples:

> Be pleased, O LORD, to deliver me!
>
> O LORD, make haste to help me!
>
> Let those be put to shame and disappointed altogether
>
> who seek to snatch away my life;
>
> let those be turned back and brought to dishonor
>
> who delight in my hurt!

Let those be appalled because of their shame
    who say to me, "Aha, Aha!" (Ps. 40:13–15)

Save me, O God!
    For the waters have come up to my neck.
I sink in deep mire,
    where there is no foothold;
I have come into deep waters,
    and the flood sweeps over me.
I am weary with my crying out;
    my throat is parched.
My eyes grow dim
    with waiting for my God. (Ps. 69:1–3)

Incline your ear, O LORD, and answer me,
    for I am poor and needy.
Preserve my life, for I am godly;
    save your servant, who trusts in you—you are my God.
Be gracious to me, O Lord,
    for to you do I cry all the day.
Gladden the soul of your servant,
    for to you, O Lord, do I lift up my soul.
For you, O Lord, are good and forgiving,
    abounding in steadfast love to all who call upon you.
Give ear, O LORD, to my prayer;
    listen to my plea for grace.
In the day of my trouble I call upon you,
    for you answer me. (Ps. 86:1–7)

I chose these three examples because they are written by David, an individual described in Scripture as "a man after [God's] heart" (1 Sam. 13:14; Acts 13:22). The Lord wants us to cry out to Him in our time of need. In fact, the Psalms are given to us as prayers and praises to claim for our own.

Another psalm of David finds a unique place in redemptive history:

> My God, my God, why have you forsaken me?
> Why are you so far from saving me, from the words of my groaning?
> O my God, I cry by day, but you do not answer,
> and by night, but I find no rest. (Ps. 22:1–2)

Jesus quoted these words on the cross in the midst of His anguish. Jesus, the perfect God-man, cried out to the Father in the depths of His suffering. He was triumphantly raised from the dead so that, among many other blessings, we can "with confidence draw near to the throne of grace, that we may receive mercy and find grace to help in time of need" (Heb. 4:16).

Have you taken time to bring your circumstances before the Lord?[17] Remember the words of Peter: "Humble yourselves, therefore, under the mighty hand of God so that at the proper time he may exalt you, casting all your anxieties on him, because he cares for you" (1 Peter 5:6–7).

---

17 See chapter 9, "If God Is Sovereign, Why Bother to Pray?"

Ask Others for Help

Third, one of the worst things that we can do in the midst of trials is to isolate ourselves from others. Paul wrote that we are to "bear one another's burdens, and so fulfill the law of Christ" (Gal. 6:2). Yes, the Lord is our ultimate burden bearer, but He has provided the church, the body of believers, so that it will come alongside to assist in our time of need. Ed Welch notes that "God's gifts to us are people—not just one person, but the church. This is how Christ meets us. The reason we need so many people is that we need Christ Himself. Since His glory and gifts are so immense, we need many people, not just an individual person."[18]

Jerry Bridges reminds us of the mutual nature of our care for one another:

> Don't just share your struggles, and above all, don't just commiserate with one another. Remember, we are to be ministers of grace to each other. We are to seek to be avenues of the Holy Spirit to help the other person appropriate the grace of God. Praying with and for one another, sharing applicable portions of Scripture, and helping each other submit to God's providential dealings with us, must characterize our times together.[19]

This captures the comprehensive care for one another that Paul described in urging us to "rejoice with those who rejoice, weep with those who weep" (Rom. 12:15). The Greek word for "fellowship"

---

18 Edward T. Welch, *Addictions: A Banquet in the Grave: Finding Hope in the Power of the Gospel* (Phillipsburg, N.J.: P&R, 2001), 252.

19 Jerry Bridges, *Transforming Grace* (Carol Stream, Ill.: NavPress, 1991), 193.

is *koinōnia*, and at the heart of its meaning is the idea of "sharing" with one another. Sharing one's joys *and* sorrows is an important element in the fellowship of believers. As we have seen the people of God rally around one another in times of immense loss, Barb and I have often wondered how people who don't have the support of others in the body of Christ cope, or even survive. Don't forget how desperately we need one another in the larger struggle. The Puritan author George Swinnock famously wrote, "Satan watcheth for those vessels that sail without a convoy."[20] Have you shared your burden with someone that you know and trust? Are you part of a body of believers through whom you can receive Christ's care? Please don't think that you can "go it alone."

Learn to Be Contented

When we talk about contentment, we are not talking about complacency—that is, an indifference to the circumstances we endure. The Apostle Paul wrote in his time of need: "I have learned in whatever situation I am to be content. I know how to be brought low, and I know how to abound. In any and every circumstance, I have learned the secret of facing plenty and hunger, abundance and need. I can do all things through him who strengthens me" (Phil. 4:11–13). He wasn't complacent. We know from his letters that he asked the churches to provide for his needs and for the needs of the suffering, but that the support was not always immediately forthcoming. Yet Paul was convinced that whatever the circumstances he was facing in God's providence, the Lord would eventually provide the required

20 George Swinnock, quoted in *A Puritan Treasury*, comp. I.D.E. Thomas (Carlisle, Pa.: Banner of Truth, 2000), 77.

resources and would grant the strength to persevere in the meantime. This is what contentment looks like. A.W. Pink points out: "Contentment, then, is the product of a heart resting in God. It is the soul's enjoyment of that peace that passes all understanding. It is the outcome of my will being brought into subjection to the Divine will. It is the blessed assurance that God does all things well, and is, even now, making all things work together for my ultimate good."[21] Can you say that you are contented right now?

Mark of a Sovereigntist: Hope

As Paul writes to the Romans: "We rejoice in hope of the glory of God. Not only that, but we rejoice in our sufferings, knowing that suffering produces endurance, and endurance produces character, and character produces hope, and hope does not put us to shame, because God's love has been poured into our hearts through the Holy Spirit who has been given to us" (Rom. 5:2–5). "Sufferings" is a word that describes a broad category of pressures we face, including persecution, affliction, distress, and tribulation. Paul knew about each of these circumstances personally, and his language focuses on the fact that in the plan of God, our sufferings are never to be seen in isolation, but when endured in faith, they will produce endurance, character, and hope. John Murray observes that Paul "has described a circle, beginning with hope and *therefore* ending with hope."[22]

What is the "hope" that provides bookends for sanctifying suffering that we endure? It is the "hope of the glory of God" (v. 2).

---

21 A.W. Pink, *Comfort for Christians* (Grand Rapids, Mich.: Baker, 1989), 85–86.

22 John Murray, *Epistle to the Romans*, NICOT (Grand Rapids, Mich.: Eerdmans, 1959), 164, emphasis original.

Once again, we are challenged to bring the vertical dimension into our thinking. What is the "glory of God" of which Paul speaks? While His glory can be defined as the majesty of God that stands apart from His creation, a few chapters later Paul tells us that the "glory of God" is not only something that we will see, but something in which we will participate. It is connected with our transformation at the coming of Jesus. The "glory of the children of God" (8:21) will come with the "redemption of our bodies" (v. 23) on that great resurrection day.[23] We can't even begin to imagine how glorious that will be! In fact, elsewhere Paul writes, "Things which eye has not seen and ear has not heard, and which have not entered the heart of man, all that God has prepared for those who love Him" (1 Cor. 2:9, NASB).[24] This progression from hope to hope is designed to strengthen us as we endure the burdens of this life. In fact, Paul declares that "the sufferings of this present time are not worth comparing with the glory that is to be revealed to us" (Rom. 8:18).

Think of the worst suffering that you have endured. Think of the burdens that you are enduring now. They are not even worth comparing to what God has prepared for you! Paul reminds us of the same point when he writes: "For this light momentary affliction is preparing for us an eternal weight of glory beyond all comparison, as we look not to the things that are seen but to the things that are unseen. For the things that are seen are transient, but the things that are unseen are eternal" (2 Cor. 4:17–18). This is the hopeful, forward-looking perspective of the sovereigntist in the midst of suffering.

---

23 Read Romans 8:18–24.

24 Quoting Isaiah 64:4.

For Further Reflection

1. Have you fallen into the trap of longing for the "good old days"? Were they really so good? What challenges existed in the good old days that you have failed to consider?
2. Have your troubles caused you to overlook God's current blessings to you? Take a moment and reflect on all that is good in your life.
3. Are you willing to accept the fact that your current struggles are being used by our loving God to complete His divine work in you?
4. How will keeping your eyes on God make a difference in what you are facing now?
5. Have you shared your burden with someone you know and trust? Are you part of a body of believers through whom you can receive Christ's care? If not, why not?

6

When the Rainbow Appears

Pressing on Afterward

"You can't see anything properly while your eyes are blurred with tears."
—C.S. Lewis

New normal is an expression that describes a new state of existence after a change in circumstances has occurred. For example, the TSA requirement to take off one's shoes as part of security screening before boarding an airplane has become the new normal ever since the "shoe bomber" attempted to blow up a plane many years ago. Or the new normal of inflation-induced strategy to shrink products while keeping the price the same or even raising it!

How are we to move forward after we have experienced hardship? What does the new normal look like for someone who has faced an unexpected loss or a traumatic event? For most people, it comes down to a choice between faith and bitterness.

Faith vs. Bitterness

In chapter 5, we looked at the hardships that Job endured, but we did not mention that these were also losses to *Job's wife*. She also lost all *her* children, to whom she had given birth and whom she had nurtured. She also had to be concerned about the loss of their herds, the loss of their livelihood. We noted that Job's response was one of faith, but what was the reaction of Job's wife? Hers was not a response of faith: "Then his wife said to him, 'Do you still hold fast your integrity? Curse God and die'" (Job 2:9). To her credit, she did not utter these words until after Job's health was ruined. We do not read any more about Job's wife after this exchange. In Job and his wife, we see two responses to the tragedies of life: faith and bitterness. Granted, they are not necessarily mutually exclusive, but if placed on a continuum, people usually gravitate toward one or the other—toward bitterness or faith.

I have seen the difference that walking by faith (or not) makes in people's lives. Late one night I received a call that the teenage son of one of our church members had been seriously injured in an accident. His car had been T-boned by another driver, who had run a stop sign. His injuries were such that he did not survive. Of course, this was a tragic and unexpected loss. The grief was overwhelming. Sadly, the young man's mother became so bitter and angry that it affected her for the rest of her life. Sometimes her anger was focused on the driver who had caused the accident, sometimes it was directed to family and friends who didn't "understand," but ultimately, it was aimed at God for what had happened. As Jerry Bridges has observed, "Bitterness arises in our hearts when we do not trust in the sovereign rule of God in our lives."[1] Scripture speaks of a "root of bitterness" that

---

1 Jerry Bridges, *The Pursuit of Holiness* (Carol Stream, Ill.: NavPress, 1996), 120.

can spring up and cause trouble (Heb. 12:15). If we allow bitterness to take root in our lives, it will grow into a wiry vine that bears all kinds of troublesome fruit that affects not only us but those around us. If you have ever indulged in a self-focused "pity party," you know that it doesn't make you feel better. Neither does it help those around you. This is where the rubber meets the road of being a sovereigntist: trusting God's plan over the long haul. Ed Welch cautions: "If we are angry [with] God . . . we should be reminded that His love is much more sophisticated than we know. Our anger shows that we are small children who think we know what is best."[2]

On the other hand, I have seen a remarkable example of living life by faith after trauma in the life of my own wife. When Barb was four years old, her father, after a fight with her mother, was killed late one night in a motorcycle accident. Her mother, against all counsel, married an ex-con, who proceeded to make life miserable for the family. He couldn't hold down a job and would give away (or throw away) food or clothing given to them. He wasn't going to "accept charity" from anyone. He would return home in a drunken stupor and beat Barb's mother in front of her eyes. She and her sister would often find safe haven at the home of their grandparents, who were doing all that they could to rescue these children from this nightmare. Children's and youth services could do nothing because whenever they would stop in for a visit, Barb's stepdad was on his best behavior, denying everything, and her mother had the home "ready for company."

Then one night Barb's stepdad got into a drunken brawl and came home in a cast. The next day he wasn't feeling well and stayed

---

2 Edward T. Welch, *Depression: Looking Up from the Stubborn Darkness* (Greensboro, N.C.: New Growth, 2011), 70.

home. It was then that her stepdad crossed the line, and finally there was enough evidence to remove Barb and her sister from the home. In addition to the trauma that she had experienced in the home, she had to testify in court against her stepfather, in his presence. By God's grace, instead of being sent to foster families, Barb and her sister were welcomed into the homes of two aunts, where they lived through their high school years. During the week of Barb's high school graduation, her beloved uncle died of cancer at only thirty-five years old. What was Barb's response to all this? She believed that she had a heavenly Father who was watching over her through the trauma of the tragic death of her father, the abuse by her stepfather, and the death of her beloved uncle.

Those who know Barb and those who meet her would never guess that she had endured such hardship. I like to say that she is a "trophy of God's grace." What carried her through was her faith in the Lord, who is sovereign over all things. Barb is a true sovereigntist, often commenting that "God doesn't waste anything, the good or the bad."

A Word about Closure

Some years ago, Dr. William Petit's Connecticut home was invaded by career criminals, who beat him into unconsciousness and tied him up in the basement. The thugs murdered his wife and two daughters and set the house on fire. The severely injured Petit regained consciousness and managed to work his way outside through a basement door, calling for help. The gruesome crime left him with deep sadness and loss. The murderers were eventually tried and found guilty in a highly publicized trial. They were also subsequently sentenced to death, after which reporters encircled the bereaved husband and father and asked him whether this brought him closure. He looked up at the reporters, both surprised and angered by the question, and replied: "I don't think there's ever closure. I think whoever came up with that concept is an imbecile, whoever they are." A year later, he was asked about it again, and Petit said that he had been "very much insulted" when asked whether a death sentence in the case would "somehow give me closure. Absolutely not."[3] Who knows the motive of the reporters in this case or of others who ask the same question of us when we have faced hardship?

People want us to be well, and they want us to be able to "move on." This is their hope for their own sake as much as for ours. If *closure* means moving on as though nothing had happened, it is wishful thinking. But if *closure* means moving forward with faith in God's sovereignty, accepting the new normal even though we don't understand the "why," it is helpful. The events that we experience through God's providence should not embitter us or make us emotional cripples. Will you always feel loss? Yes. Will you always wonder "why?" Yes. Will you ever "get over it"? No, at least not in the sense that your loss will seem to have never happened. But the sovereigntist will move forward, leaning on the everlasting arms for every step.

A Grief Observed

C.S. Lewis offers an intimate look at his own path from the darkness of grief to the light of hope. Lewis lost his wife after a battle with cancer. He was with her through it all to the end. Together they shared the ups

3 ABC News, "No 'Closure' for Petit despite Death Sentence Ruling," November 9, 2010, https://abcnews.go.com/Health/StressCoping/dr-william-petit-steven-hayes-death-penalty-closure/story?id=12103364.

and downs of brief remissions and times of hope. Finally, she passed into glory. In the wake of her death, Lewis recorded his thoughts in several notebooks, which were not written for the purpose of publication, but "on reading through some of them later, he felt that they might be of some help to others who were similarly afflicted with the turmoil of thought and feeling which grief forces upon us."[4]

Entering the pages of *A Grief Observed*, one finds a grief-stricken man in full survival mode. Even his faith is tested as he writes:

> Meanwhile, where is God? This is one of the most disquieting symptoms. When you are happy, so happy that you have no sense of needing Him, so happy that you are tempted to feel His claims upon you as an interruption, if you remember yourself and turn to Him with gratitude and praise, you will be—or so it feels—welcomed with open arms. But go to Him when your need is desperate, when all other help is vain, and what do you find? A door slammed in your face, and a sound of bolting and double bolting on the inside. After that, silence.[5]

This is certainly the way that we can feel in our grief when we are experiencing all that comes with it, including fatigue, disorientation, and even doubt. All this, including bitterness, is expressed in Lewis' notebooks. But after heartfelt wrestling in heart and mind, he acknowledges, "And so, perhaps, with God, I have gradually been coming to feel that the door is no longer shut and bolted."[6]

---

4 Douglas Gresham, introduction to *A Grief Observed* by C.S. Lewis (New York: HarperCollins, 1961), xxvi–xxvii. Gresham was Lewis' stepson.

5 Lewis, *A Grief Observed*, 5–6.

6 Lewis, *A Grief Observed*, 46.

Yes, grief is a process. Don't be surprised if your sadness is mixed with anger, but don't expect all your questions to be answered, either. An intellect like Lewis had lots of questions that were not to be answered: "When I lay these questions before God I get no answer. But a rather special 'No answer.' It is not the locked door. It is more like a silent, certainly not uncompassionate, gaze. As though He shook His head not in refusal but waiving the question. Like, 'Peace, child; you don't understand.'"[7]

An earlier observation in Lewis' notebooks sheds light on the disorientation that he felt and that we often feel: "You can't see anything properly while your eyes are blurred with tears."[8] Yes, for the believer there is not only light at the end of the tunnel but light *in* the tunnel because despite how you *feel*, He is with you: "Yea, though I walk through the valley of the shadow of death, I will fear no evil: for thou art with me" (Ps. 23:4, KJV). "If I say, 'Surely the darkness shall cover me, and the light about me be night,' even the darkness is not dark to you; the night is bright as the day, for darkness is as light with you" (Ps. 139:11–12). Lewis' ultimate comfort was in the knowledge that his wife was with the Lord. He remembered her final words: "She said not to me but to the chaplain, 'I am at peace with God.' She smiled, but not at me."[9]

Dealing with the "Why?" Question

When hardship comes, our ability to move from the storm into a calmer season of life depends on how we deal with the question that

7 Lewis, *A Grief Observed*, 69.

8 Lewis, *A Grief Observed*, 45.

9 Lewis, *A Grief Observed*, 76.

arises, either spoken or unspoken: "Why?" Why did this happen to my loved one? Why did this happen to me? Why did this happen at all? If God works all things according to the counsel of His will, why this? As we observed in chapter 5, "Why?" with a capital *W* is a question about the secret plan of God, and we are likely never to know the answer in our lifetime. But the Scriptures reveal several answers to the question "why?" spelled with a lowercase *w*. We are told that God allows suffering in our lives for several reasons.

God Uses Suffering to Strengthen Us

James brings a remarkable perspective: "Count it all joy, my brothers, when you meet trials of various kinds, for you know that the testing of your faith produces steadfastness. And let steadfastness have its full effect, that you may be perfect and complete, lacking in nothing" (James 1:2–4). James is making the same point that Paul was making in Romans 5:2–5, that our sufferings strengthen us. James says that our trials produce "steadfastness." Though the ESV translators used different words in each context, the Greek word for "steadfastness" is the same.[10]

It's one thing to trust God through trials, but to endure them joyfully is another thing entirely. Facing trials with joy is definitely counterintuitive. But the biblical logic is quite compelling. Since all things come to us from the all-wise hand of God, and if all things work together for good, and if God is using them, our circumstances can be considered to be joy. The verb translated "consider" means to "reckon as" or to "deem as." The idea is that whatever occurs, it is to be placed in the "joy" column.

---

10 Greek *hypomonēn*.

This is a choice that we are called to make every day, isn't it? Imagine what a difference it would make in your life if, through the power of the Holy Spirit, you chose to put your difficulties in the joy column because you knew that God was at work through them to make you stronger.

Sometimes the Lord Uses Suffering to Draw Us Nearer to Him

The longest chapter in the Bible is Psalm 119. In the psalm, there are twenty-two sections consisting of eight verses each, totaling 176 verses. The psalm's uniqueness is found in that the verses in each of the twenty-two sections begin with a successive letter of the Hebrew alphabet. For example, the first eight verses begin with the letter aleph, the second eight begin with beth, and so on throughout the psalm. In other words, it is an acrostic. The psalm is devoted in its entirety to the beauty, dignity, and usefulness of the Scriptures. In verse 67, the writer exclaims, "Before I was afflicted I went astray, but now I keep your word." The Hebrew verb translated "astray" is used of sin: of straying from the way of God, straying from the Word of God. The writer doesn't tell us what the sin was or how far he strayed, but he does tell us that the Lord used affliction to bring him back. Neither is the specific affliction identified. For an example of how the word is used in the Bible, in both Genesis 15:13 and Exodus 1:11–12 it describes the pressure and persecution brought on the people of God when they were enslaved in Egypt. What was the result? "Their cry for rescue from slavery came up to God" (Ex. 2:23), and God answered their cry.

Have you ever noticed that the trials that you have been called to endure have drawn you nearer to the Lord? Perhaps your suffering actually opened your eyes to your need for Him. In my ministry, I have seen this several times. In many situations, individuals diagnosed with an affliction that would eventually take their lives called out to the Lord. They found peace and forgiveness with Him before they were called to stand before Him face-to-face. There was once a man who was a relative of a church member and attended services when he was in town. He came because his relatives came. They always sat in the front row, and his body language was clear: "I'd rather be anywhere else than here." A few years later, he was diagnosed with cancer, and I went to visit him in the hospital. He asked me whether "they," meaning his relatives, had asked me to come. I had to honestly answer, "Yes." After some uncomfortable small talk, I asked, "Would you prefer that I hadn't come?" to which he said, "Yes." I prayed a brief prayer for him and exited. Over time, as the cancer progressed, his heart softened as he was confronted with his mortality, and he trusted Jesus as his Savior. I led his funeral service, during which I had the joy of relating his progression from a hardened skeptic to a sincere believer in Jesus.

Of course, the afflictions that we endure are not all life-or-death. It appears that the suffering of the psalmist was not potentially life-ending. But the message is that sometimes in His wisdom, the Lord uses hardship to draw us nearer to Himself. Just a few verses later, the psalmist writes, "It is good for me that I was afflicted, that I might learn your statutes" (Ps. 119:71). In hindsight, he can say that since the affliction led him to understand God's Word, he can see that it was good. Being drawn to His statutes through difficulties is drawing us nearer to Him. Anything that draws us nearer to Him is good!

Sometimes God Uses Our Suffering to Equip Us to Comfort Others

In Paul's second letter to the Corinthians, he reminds his readers that when we suffer, God is the primary Comforter: "Blessed be the God and Father of our Lord Jesus Christ, the Father of mercies and God of all comfort, who comforts us in all our affliction" (2 Cor. 1:3–4). When we suffer, we must first look to the Chief Comforter, who is also the Chief Sufferer. The word translated "affliction" is the same word that Paul uses in his earlier comment to the Roman church about how God uses various "sufferings" in our lives. Notice the comprehensiveness of God's care and comfort toward us in *all* our affliction. There is *nothing* that is excluded.

Paul goes on to reveal that a purpose behind God's comfort toward us is "so that we may be able to comfort those who are in any affliction, with the comfort with which we ourselves are comforted by God" (v. 4). Now the comfort shifts from a vertical direction to the horizontal. The comfort that we have received from God we now share with one another. It is remarkable that the language is identical, indicating "any affliction." Did you ever think that God's plan for you has included suffering so that you can comfort others who may be suffering in the same way? In an earlier chapter, I mentioned a dear family who lost their teenage daughter suddenly and unexpectedly. To be honest, it was a traumatic experience not just for the family but also for the church. Just a few months later, another family in the church lost their dear son to SIDS.[11] His death was also sudden and unexpected. I arranged for the mother of the teenager who had died to meet with the mother of the little boy who had passed. It was quite an amazing conversation between these two grieving moms, and it was remarkable to have the privilege of eavesdropping as the one mom shared with the newly bereaved mom about how she lives through each day and how God helps her in her grief. A bond

11 Sudden infant death syndrome.

between these women, sealed by shared suffering, enabled them both to benefit from the conversation. It wasn't that I as their pastor wasn't able to be of help, but the women had a unique experience of affliction that I had never had.

Whatever affliction God might have allowed in His providence in your life, look for opportunities to share with others who have similarly suffered. Also, if you are suffering, first of all look to the comfort of the Lord, who promises, "Blessed are those who mourn, for they shall be comforted" (Matt. 5:4). But also be on the alert for those who may be going through the same or similar difficulties. This is one of the blessings of being part of the body of Christ.

For God's Glory

We have already seen the remarkable promise that God works all things together for good to those who love Him (see Rom. 8:28), but even that assurance is subordinate to a higher answer to the question "Why?" The ultimate purpose behind everything that God does is that He will be glorified. Paul writes: "For from him and through him and to him are all things. To him be glory forever. Amen" (11:36). Earlier we spoke of how the glory of God will be manifested *in* us at the coming of Jesus, but *everything* is designed by God to bring Him glory. This is often difficult to see when we are in the middle of hardship.

Jesus had a dear friend named Lazarus who was not well.[12] His sisters sent word to Jesus that His friend was gravely ill. In hearing the news, Jesus said: "This illness does not lead to death. It is for the glory of God, so that the Son of God may be glorified through it"

---

12 Read the story in its entirety in John 11.

(John 11:4). But when Jesus arrived, Lazarus had already been dead for four days. His sisters were upset because they were convinced that if Jesus had been there, their brother and His friend would not have died. Jesus had another plan. He comforted Mary and Martha and said, "Did I not tell you that if you believed you would see the glory of God?" (v. 40). How was God going to be glorified through this? In a scene that is one of the most dramatic in all Scripture, Jesus went to the tomb, had the stone rolled away from the entrance, and said, "Lazarus, come out" (v. 43). Lazarus came out! God was glorified, and the authenticating miracle proved that Jesus was the resurrection and the life. The promise of Jesus to be the source of life is not always demonstrated immediately, as it was in the case of Lazarus. Neither is the glory of God always so clearly seen.

Sometimes God is glorified in the way that His people respond to crises that might endure for years, decades, or even a lifetime. I have dear friends, Ken and Nancy, whose firstborn was diagnosed with Down syndrome. Immediately after Keith's birth, the physician said, "Get the child out of the arms of his mother as soon as possible and place him in a state institution."[13] His mother's first words were, "We will raise this child as any other child." Ken recalls that "in the moments of silence that followed, we knew only two things for certain: The condition was irreversible, and God knew about it."[14] All of us who have known this family have been blessed by their trust in God's sovereign plan and their determination to glorify Him. Ken writes, "Now, more than fifty years later, we realize that we may never

---

13 Kenneth Laudermilch, *Designed, No Less* (Murrells Inlet, S.C.: Covenant, 2020), 14.

14 Laudermilch, 14.

know his complete purpose in designing Keith with an extra chromosome, but we have experienced enough to know that at least part of his plan was to create Keith as a conduit to display to us and others his love and grace."[15] One of Keith's favorite questions to ask is, "Do you love Jesus?" In his life, Keith and his family glorify God and point others to the One who is the source of abundant and eternal life.

Whether your afflictions are short-lived or lifelong, have you considered how God is glorified through them? The answer might not emerge immediately or easily as you think retrospectively, but ponder how you might give glory to God through them now and in the coming days. Ultimately, the answer to the "Why?" question is left to the wise providence of God.

Mark of the Sovereigntist: Joy

We saw in James 1:2 that when we go through trials, we should "count it all joy." If that is the case, our lives should surely be characterized by joy when the storm passes, and every day. George Muller was a nineteenth-century minister who was best known for establishing orphanages in Bristol, England. He had an amazing perspective on daily life in the Lord: "I saw more clearly than ever, that the first great and primary business to which I ought to attend every day was, to have my soul happy in the Lord. The first thing to be concerned about was not, how much I might serve the Lord, how I might glorify the Lord; but how I might get my soul into a happy state, and how my inner man might be nourished."[16] He saw being

15 Laudermilch, 14.

16 *The Autobiography of George Muller* (New Kensington, Pa.: Whitaker House, 1996), 55.

"happy" in the Lord as a prerequisite for living and for serving the Lord every day.

Sometimes we think of the Apostle Paul as an austere figure, but he was a man who knew the joy of the Lord and told the Philippian church, "Rejoice in the Lord always; again I will say, rejoice" (Phil. 4:4). He didn't say, "Rejoice sometimes" or "Rejoice when things are good," but he said, "Rejoice in the Lord always"! What's remarkable about these words is that Paul wrote them while he was imprisoned in Rome. In fact, Philippians is Paul's most joyful letter: he speaks of joy and rejoicing more than a dozen times in its four short chapters.

John MacArthur reminds us that it is important to clarify the meaning of Christian joy: "Christian joy is not a giddy, superficial happiness that can be devastated by illness, economic difficulties, broken relationships, or the countless other vicissitudes and disappointments of life. Instead, it flows from the deep, unshakable confidence that God is eternally in control of every aspect of life for the good of His beloved children—a confidence rooted in the knowledge of His Word."[17] There you have it. We can be filled with joy because we know that God is at work in the world and in us, accomplishing His purpose. If you know Jesus Christ, your sins are forgiven and you are going to heaven, and that fact is the same today, tomorrow, and forever.

One day as I was entering our church office, our administrative assistant asked, "Are you always up?" My answer: "Yes, because I'm going to heaven!" But it is not so much an emotion or affect as it is a settled perspective based on an unshakable truth that will never change because it is grounded in His promises.

---

17 John MacArthur, *2 Corinthians* (Chicago: Moody, 2003), 484.

The very fact that people were receiving His message brought Jesus joy. After His disciples returned from a fruitful preaching mission, Jesus "*rejoiced* in the Holy Spirit and said, 'I thank you, Father, Lord of heaven and earth, that you have hidden these things from the wise and understanding and revealed them to little children; yes, Father, for such was your gracious will'" (Luke 10:21, emphasis added). The writer of Hebrews urges us to keep "looking to Jesus, the founder and perfecter of our faith, who for the joy that was set before him endured the cross, despising the shame, and is seated at the right hand of the throne of God" (Heb. 12:2–3). It is likely that the prospect of His mission's being accomplished in the salvation of His people brought Him a depth of joy that motivated Him the whole way through the cross, the resurrection, and the ascension into heaven. He wants you to walk in His joy every day, whether the season of life for you is cloudy, stormy, or clear. His desire is that His "joy may be in you, and that your joy may be full" (John 15:11).

How is this possible? It is not something that you conjure up or "fake." If you recall, "joy" is the second aspect of the fruit of the Spirit, right after "love." It is a settled perspective anchored in God's truth, empowered by His Spirit, flowing through your life whatever each day brings.

This is God's desire for you. King Solomon, as he thought about living life "under the sun" or, as I have suggested, in the seasons of life, wrote, "I perceived that there is nothing better for them than to be joyful and to do good as long as they live; also that everyone should eat and drink and take pleasure in all his toil—this is God's gift to man" (Eccl. 3:12–13).

A Matter of Perspective

Having considered the seasons of life in which we are called to trust our sovereign God, I have an important question for you: "Do you really believe that the skies in your seasons of life will always be sunny and clear?" Perhaps you believe that this is the best of all possible worlds? If so, you are doomed to a life of frustration, despair, and disappointment. This leads to a worldview reality check.

The Scriptures have a *realistic* view of the world. It is a world that has been affected by the first couple's rebellion against their Creator. It is a world, and humanity with it, that has "fallen" from its original pristine beauty and holiness. What does that look like? First of all, humanity is in bondage to sin. Why do people do what they do? Why do crooks prey on old people? How could someone sexually abuse a child? Why do I need protection on everything I own, from my car to my house to my identity? Why do people hate other people? Why are people prejudiced? I could go on and on, but the answer, put in scriptural terms, is that "all have sinned and fall short of the glory of God" (Rom. 3:23). All of us have sinful natures that make us self-centered and self-interested. Ordinarily, when someone says, "I'm only human," it isn't a statement of confident integrity but a confession of weakness and vulnerability with which every human identifies. I would guess that a lot of the angst that you have in your life is brought on by other people.

But let's not forget the angst that *you* bring into the lives of others. This is why we need Jesus, who died and rose again so that our sins can be forgiven and so that we can have a new power to live a new life. He breaks our bondage to sin and turns our selfish hearts of stone into hearts that are alive to love God and others. This is why

you sin, and this is why humanity is such a mess. But that's not all. Jesus makes an important clarification about suffering and sin. He makes it clear that there is not a one-to-one correlation between our suffering and something we have done. He disabused His own disciples of that notion when they asked Him about a man born blind:[18] "Rabbi, who sinned, this man or his parents, that he was born blind?" (John 9:2). The thinking at the time was that God was running the world in a tit-for-tat fashion in which if you suffered, you must have done something wrong. Listen to Jesus' reply: "It was not that this man sinned, or his parents, but that the works of God might be displayed in him" (v. 3).

Granted, there are times when specific pain can be linked to a specific sin—for example, the suffering brought on when a drunk driver plows head-on into an oncoming car and kills its unsuspecting occupants. Or the pain that comes into a marriage when a spouse commits adultery. We must remember, however, that sin is plenary in the hearts of all people and that human suffering is the result. This is the reason that C.S. Lewis notes, "A Christian cannot, therefore, believe any of those who promise that if only some reform in our economic, political, or hygienic system were made, a heaven on earth will follow."[19] But that's not all.

The first couple's sin also affected creation. The Lord said: "Cursed is the ground because of you; in pain you shall eat of it all the days of your life; thorns and thistles it shall bring forth for you; and you shall eat the plants of the field. By the sweat of your face

---

18 Read the remarkable account in John 9.

19 C.S. Lewis, *The Problem of Pain* (1940; repr., New York: HarperOne, 1996), 114–15.

you shall eat bread" (Gen. 3:17–19). Work is going to be really hard because the earth will not give up its harvest easily. Paul echoes this idea when he writes, "For the creation was subjected to futility," and "we know that the whole creation has been groaning together in the pains of childbirth until now" (Rom. 8:20, 22).

Do you wonder why the natural world is in such an upheaval? How do you explain all the floods, earthquakes, tsunamis, and hurricanes? How do you explain plagues and pandemics? It is because the natural world is buckling under the weight of the moral failure of humanity. But Paul's argument is designed to point to the only hope for humanity and creation: Jesus Christ. When He returns, "the creation itself will be set free from its bondage to corruption and obtain the freedom of the glory of the children of God" (v. 21). When He returns, His followers will be revealed in glory to be His children, and there will be a new heaven and earth. *That* is when the best of all possible worlds will be revealed. This is the reason that a sovereigntist is an *optimistic* realist. In the meantime, Jesus told His disciples: "In the world you will have tribulation. But take heart; I have overcome the world" (John 16:33). Jesus wants us to enter life with a realistic worldview and wants us to know that He is there to deliver us.

For Further Reflection

1. Would you say that your response to hardship is bitterness or faith? Are you willing to trust God when you don't understand the reason that something has happened?
2. Can you think of some ways that the Lord has used difficulties in your life to make you stronger?

3. Can you think of some ways that the Lord has used difficulties in your life to bring Him glory?
4. Would you consider yourself to be a joyful person? Given what the Lord has done for you, is there any reason that you shouldn't be joyful every day?

Part Three

SPECIAL CHALLENGES IN THE SEASONS OF LIFE

7

Sovereign Help in Times of Temptation

"No temptation has overtaken you
that is not common to man."
(1 Cor. 10:13)

One of the daily challenges that we face is temptation. A prayer that we have been instructed to pray by our Lord is "Lead us not into temptation, but deliver us from evil" (Matt. 6:13). Being a believer in Jesus Christ does not exempt us from temptation. Consider the fact that our Lord Himself was subject to temptation, but that He triumphed over the evil one. In this fallen world, in our fallen natures, you can be sure that temptation will come.

How does the truth of God's sovereignty help in times of temptation? First, let's be clear that God is not the *source* of temptation. James exhorts: "Let no one say when he is tempted, 'I am being tempted by God,' for God cannot be tempted with evil, and he himself tempts no one. But each person is tempted when he is lured and enticed by his own desire. Then desire when it has conceived gives birth to sin, and sin when it is fully grown brings forth death" (James 1:13–15).

Second, the only temptation that comes into your life is something that has been *allowed* by God. Philip Ryken states: "The fact that God does not tempt us does not mean that our temptations are somehow outside of His control. God is sovereign over all the affairs of life, including every temptation to sin. Although He does not cause our temptations, He does allow them to occur."[1] You will notice that temptations were part of God's plan for His Son. Immediately after Jesus was baptized, the Spirit descended on Him, and a voice from heaven said, "This is my beloved Son, with whom I am well pleased" (Matt. 3:17). Instead of the accolades that one might expect to follow such a declaration, Jesus was "led up by the Spirit into the wilderness to be tempted by the devil" (4:1). It was the devil who did the tempting but the sovereign Spirit who led Jesus into the wilderness.

Why was this necessary? The writer of the book of Hebrews tells us: "For we do not have a high priest who is unable to sympathize with our weaknesses, but one who in every respect has been tempted as we are, yet without sin. Let us then with confidence draw near to the throne of grace, that we may receive mercy and find grace to help in time of need" (Heb. 4:15–16). In order to become our High Priest, He had to experience what we would experience, yet without sin. To put it in another way, no temptation has come to you that didn't come to Jesus first. No temptation has come to you that Jesus did not resist and overcome. What does that mean to you? It is not

---

1 Philip Graham Ryken, *When You Pray: Making the Lord's Prayer Your Own* (Wheaton, Ill.: Crossway, 2000), 151.

that Jesus merely sympathizes with you as a distant onlooker but that He provides "mercy and . . . grace to help in time of need." Jesus is in a unique position to help you.

Our son was a scout platoon commander with the United States Army during Operation Iraqi Freedom, specifically during "the surge," which was the strategic turning point of the war. It was also the most dangerous and deadly season for coalition forces. Nate's platoon was engaged in clearing hundreds of buildings and often engaged Al-Qaeda soldiers and sympathizers. He asked his commanding officer for some additional tools to accomplish his mission. He requested a sniper rifle and a TOW[2] missile system. The TOW system would enable his platoon to respond to a threat immediately, rather than waiting for air support to arrive. His commanding officer denied his request. When I asked him for the CO's reason for denying the request, Nate said, "Dad, he denied it because he didn't have any combat experience." Dear believer, please know that your Commanding Officer has "combat experience." He knows what you are going through because He went through it Himself and was victorious over the diabolical tempter and over all temptations. In union with Him through the Spirit He has given, we can have the will and the strength to be victorious, too. Remember that "he who is in you is greater than he who is in the world" (1 John 4:4).

Earlier in the letter, the writer to the Hebrews also reminds us that "because he himself has suffered when tempted, he is able to help those who are being tempted" (Heb. 2:18). This is a powerful reminder that Jesus "suffered" when He was tempted. Sometimes we think that since Jesus was the God-man, resisting temptation was

---

2 Heavy Tube-Launched, Optically Tracked, Wireless-Guided.

"easy" for Him. It was not. Temptation was a source of suffering for Jesus, too. Remember when you are suffering under the burden of temptation that Jesus also suffered. In this, He identifies with you. By God's grace, ask the Lord to enable you to identify with Him.

Temptation: A Promise of Help from Your Sovereign God

To be even more specific in seeing God's sovereign help given to us when we are tempted, let's look at a wonderful promise in Paul's first letter to the Corinthian church: "No temptation has overtaken you that is not common to man. God is faithful, and he will not let you be tempted beyond your ability, but with the temptation he will also provide the way of escape, that you may be able to endure it" (1 Cor. 10:13). Several principles are found in this promise.

There Is Nothing Extraordinary about Your Temptation

First, for every temptation that you experience, someone else has experienced it—and someone is probably experiencing it right now. Sometimes we get into a "woe is me" pity party, feeling that no one has ever been tempted like this before. To put Paul's words another way, "every temptation you are experiencing has been experienced by somebody else." So there is nothing out of the ordinary about your temptation. The temptation to lie? Someone else has experienced that. The temptation to steal? Someone else has experienced that one, too. Your fleshly desires are tempting you to act out in sinful ways? That's a very common one. You name it; it's been experienced by others. If we convince ourselves that our temptation is unique, we can rationalize that it is irresistible. But we have already seen that Jesus has been tempted in the same way and has prevailed.

God Is Faithful in Not Allowing You to Be Tempted beyond What You Are Able

Second, you are *never* in a position in which sinful failure is the inevitable outcome. Of course, the ability that is spoken of is not just human willpower but the power of the Spirit at work in you. You have been given every resource that you need to withstand whatever comes your way. What resources do you have? You have the promises of God, including the one that we are highlighting now. You have the Spirit of Christ indwelling you, if you are a believer. You have the support and encouragement of the community of faith, who might share the same struggle.

It should be added at this point that if you are not a believer in Jesus Christ, you don't have a chance against temptation. You don't have the Holy Spirit, you don't have an ultimate desire to please God, and you have no clue as to the potential damage that the sin you are about to commit will do to you and to those around you. I urge you to consider Jesus, who conquered temptation and death itself for all who will believe.

There Is Always a Way of Escape

Third, there is always a way out. What an amazing promise! Veterans of temptation *know* that there is an escape. The key is to *take it.* As Ed Welch puts it: "When a serpent comes across your path speaking lies, you should run from it or kill it. You shouldn't sit around for a friendly chat."[3]

---

3 Edward T. Welch, *Addictions: A Banquet in the Grave: Finding Hope in the Power of the Gospel* (Phillipsburg, N.J.: P&R, 2001), 239.

The classic scriptural example of taking the way of escape is Joseph.[4] While he served as the chief steward of Potiphar's household, his wife tried to seduce Joseph on several occasions. Finally, a day came when Joseph and Potiphar's wife were alone in the house, and she grabbed hold of him, begging him to sleep with her. What did he do? Did he rationalize by saying to himself, "No one will ever know" or "Just this once"? No, he ran, he literally ran, leaving his garment behind. He saw the way of escape and took it. In the story's context, we are given insight into Joseph's thinking in the matter. He would not give in because doing so would demonstrate disloyalty and ingratitude to Potiphar, who had given him so much. But most significant was Joseph's realization that such behavior would be a sin against God. He said, "How then can I do this great wickedness and sin against God?" (Gen. 39:9). Of course, Joseph's rejection of Potiphar's wife led to her false accusations of sexual advance, which led to his being thrown into prison.

On the other side of the "will to escape" was King David. Instead of looking for the way of escape when tempted by the sight of a beautiful woman bathing on her balcony across the way, he dove headlong into adultery.[5] He could well have ignored what he saw, but instead he allowed his passion to prevail as he called for her to be brought to him. Then he added murder to his transgression, trying to cover it up by ordering the woman's husband to be rushed to the front lines of battle, where he was sure to be killed. But God had a plan even in this.

Returning to the relevance of God's sovereignty to all this, can't you see that this promise would not be possible at all if God weren't

4 Read the full story in Genesis 39.

5 See 2 Samuel 11.

absolutely sovereign? We made this same point in chapter 2. If He weren't sovereign over *all things*, He could not *guarantee* that the temptations you face will be manageable for you with the resources He has provided. If He weren't sovereign, something might slip into your life while He wasn't looking that is completely impossible for you to handle. If He weren't sovereign over all things, He could not guarantee that there would *always* be a way of escape. If He weren't the Ruler of all circumstances, you could not be sure that a scenario wouldn't arise in which you were cornered, with no way out. No, there is *always* a way out because He has promised that it will be there. This is where human responsibility enters. Bryan Chapell stresses: "We should not assume that, because God promises to provide a way out of temptation, we have no role in our own rescue. God always provides a way of escape, but he may also require great effort from us. We take advantage of the way of escape God provides by exerting every resource he gives us to fight the enemy."[6]

Dimensions of Resistance

It is helpful to remember the threefold defense against giving in to temptation that helped Joseph. First, he was aware of the *horizontal* dimension of his life. He knew that taking Potiphar's wife would be disloyal to his boss and would lead to serious consequences. Every sin we commit has a horizontal, relational dimension, either directly or indirectly. When temptation comes, think about the impact that your sin could have on your loved ones, on your coworkers, on your reputation. As someone once said, "Satan is very good in presenting

---

6 Bryan Chapell, *Holiness by Grace: Delighting in the Joy That Is Our Strength* (Wheaton, Ill.: Crossway, 2001), 102.

the bait but hiding the hook." The enemy of our soul would hide these dimensions of the impact of our sin. Of course, he is also eager to hide the "way of escape."

Second, Joseph reminded himself of the *vertical* dimension of his sin: that his sin was against God Almighty. While in the midst of temptation, we are helped by keeping both perspectives in mind. Being confronted by Nathan with the vertical dimension of his sin is what struck David with heartfelt conviction. What was David's immediate reaction to Nathan's words? "David said to Nathan, 'I have sinned *against the Lord*'" (2 Sam. 12:13, emphasis added). He had sinned against his wives, against his subjects, against Bathsheba, against Uriah, but the primary focus of his guilt was his sin against the Lord. Even this one referred to as "a man after my heart" (Acts 13:22) was blinded by temptation to the vertical dimension of his thoughts and actions.

A third element that combines the vertical and the horizontal dimensions is the use of the "sword of the Spirit," the Word of God (Eph. 6:17). Though Joseph didn't quote Scripture verbatim, it is clear that he knew the law of God and determined not to violate it. Do you recall how Jesus responded to the devil's temptations in the wilderness?[7] Did He say, "Don't you know who I am?" No, He responded to all three temptations by quoting the Scriptures. After the second temptation, the devil saw that Jesus was countering him with Scripture, so the sneaky deceiver tried quoting Scripture himself to lure Jesus into his trap. Jesus saw right through it and countered the temptation with Scripture. The knowledge of God's truth empowered by the Spirit is a mighty weapon against temptation.

7 Read Luke's account of the wilderness temptation in Luke 4:1–12.

Jerry Bridges writes, "Our reason, enlightened by the Holy Spirit through the Word of God, stands in the way of sin gaining mastery over us through our desires."[8] Arm yourself for the battle! Take some time to find the Scripture references that apply directly to the specific temptations that you face and memorize them.

Peter urges us to "be sober-minded; be watchful. Your adversary the devil prowls around like a roaring lion, seeking someone to devour" (1 Peter 5:8). James adds, "Resist the devil, and he will flee from you" (James 4:7). Peter wisely tells us to "be watchful." Through the power of the Holy Spirit and grounded in His Word, resist! The promise is that the devil will flee. Satan is a sneak. Arthur Pink comments, "It is when we have received some special mark of the Lord's favor, or immediately after we have enjoyed some unusual season of communion with Him, that we need most to be on our guard!"[9] Luke closes his account of the temptation of our Lord with these words: "And when the devil had ended every temptation, he departed from him until an opportune time" (Luke 4:13). He wasn't finished with Jesus. He will not be finished with you and with me until we meet the Lord someday.

One More Thing: Failure Is Not Final

Have you really made a mess of things? Do you think that there is no hope for you? Do you think that you have failed so badly that God has "washed his hands" of you? I remember getting the news that a close college friend of mine who had become not only a minister but an effective church planter up and left his wife and three small

8 Jerry Bridges, *The Pursuit of Holiness* (Carol Stream, Ill.: NavPress, 1996), 64.

9 Arthur W. Pink, *Gleanings in Genesis* (Chicago: Moody, 1950), 174.

children to pursue an online connection, which became an adulterous affair.[10] He packed up, moved out, and drove away, devastating his family, shocking his church, and stunning his community. Bill had determined that this was the action he would take some months earlier. It was not a question of "if" but "when." His online "relationship" moved from cyberadultery to physical adultery. He had taken the bait but failed to see the painful hook.

There were things along the way that God was already using to convict Bill of his sin. When he had finished packing up to depart, he sat down with his wife and children to tell them that he was leaving. What was his wife's response? "I love you. I forgive you. I am praying for you." It wasn't a bitter diatribe filled with threats, which he might have expected and deserved, but it was the love of God flowing through her to her prodigal husband. These words were prominent in his mind as he was driving away from his family and his ministry. He was gone for thirteen days. When he called home during that time, his wife reminded him that she loved him and forgave him. Though he was gone for only thirteen days, his departure from his family and his God had begun much earlier. But now he "came to himself" and realized that the grass wasn't greener on the other side. He came home in answer to his wife's and his church's prayers.

But Bill had really made a mess of things. He was disciplined by his ecclesial body and removed from his position in the church. He discovered that there wasn't much of a job market for a former minister in his mid-forties with no other discernible skills. He stocked shelves,

---

10 This information is based on my personal correspondence; I have received permission to include it here. For the sake of anonymity, I am referring to my friend as "Bill."

worked in a factory, and served in a local service agency for a couple of years. Needless to say, there were very clear financial consequences that deeply affected his growing family. But he sincerely repented, and his relationship with the Lord and his family was restored.

When we really mess up, we may find it difficult to forgive ourselves. After Bill's repentance and reconciliation with his family, he met a pastoral friend for lunch and began to tearfully explain how he couldn't overcome the harm and difficulties that he had brought onto others. His friend very sternly replied, "Stop beating yourself up!" Bill was first stunned by this but then realized that "it was just what I needed. I had (without realizing it) slipped into thinking that somehow I was going to be atoning for my own sin. I was reminded that Christ had already done that, and to rest in Him alone." Yes, there are the sad consequences of sin, but never forget that the Lord's complete forgiveness is available to the repentant sinner.

In fact, the Good Shepherd Himself seeks for the stray sheep. Isn't this what the parable of the good shepherd is all about?[11] How many sheep need to be missing for the good shepherd to notice? Only one. Does the shepherd say, "Well, I've still got ninety-nine; I'll just let that one suffer the consequences"? No, the text says that the shepherd left the ninety-nine to find the lost sheep: "And if he finds it, truly, I say to you, he rejoices over it more than over the ninety-nine that never went astray. So it is not the will of my Father who is in heaven that one of these little ones should perish" (Matt. 18:13–14). The Lord seeks lost sheep, rejoices when they are found, and is determined not to lose *any* who truly belong to Him. The Lord sought straying David through the words of Nathan the prophet, and though there were

11 You can find the parable in Matthew 18:10–14.

temporal consequences of his actions, he was forgiven and restored. After His resurrection, Jesus returned to the Sea of Galilee to restore Peter after he had denied his Lord three times. He continues to seek and restore straying sheep. Are you among them? Perhaps He is seeking you through these words right now. Will you repent and believe that Jesus will forgive and restore you?

Some years later, Bill was talking with his oldest son, who had turned eighteen and was about to go off to college. He expressed his gratitude for his son's forgiveness but again shared his sorrow for all the pain that the family had suffered. Here is how Bill describes the conversation:

> His response caught me by surprise. He said, "But Dad, look at all the good that has come out of it!" He told me that if that awful event hadn't come about, he wouldn't have eventually experienced some amazing blessings. He went on to talk about the Christian girl he had met, his future at college, and the new friends and positive experiences that had come his way. I was heartened. God's Word and good news is indeed true: "Where sin increased, grace abounded all the more!" (Rom. 5:20)

Dear friend, your sovereign God works even through your failures to accomplish His perfect plan. Since God is sovereign, though not all things *are* good, all things, even your failures, work together *for* good.

Mark of a Sovereigntist: Spirit-Empowered Obedience

In His battle against the devil's temptations in the wilderness, Jesus not only knew the Scriptures and quoted the Scriptures but *obeyed* the Scriptures. He has given us the Scriptures together with the presence and power of the Holy Spirit so that when the inflection point comes in the time of temptation, we will yield to the Spirit and obey our Lord. Obedience is yielding our wills to His will in the moment when the pressure of temptation is greatest. What is our motivation? R.C. Sproul writes that our obedience "is not to be done slavishly, out of servile fear or out of some rigid, stoical desire for rule-keeping, but rather from a profound desire to express our love for the Father."[12] Our obedience is not designed to *earn* a place in God's family but serves to reveal that we *already are* God's children through faith in Jesus. Ancient church father John Chrysostom wrote, "If you knew how quickly people will forget about you after your death, you will not seek to please anyone in this life but God."

For Further Reflection

1. Reflect on the fact that Jesus was tempted in every way that we are, but without sin. Have you ever thought about the fact that Jesus "suffered" while being tempted? How does this give you hope and comfort as you face temptation?
2. How is the promise in 1 Corinthians 10:13 possible only if God is sovereign?
3. When tempted, have you ever rationalized that there was something unique and therefore irresistible about your temptation?

---

12 R.C. Sproul, *The Purpose of God: An Exposition of Ephesians* (Fearn, Scotland: Christian Focus, 1994), 123.

4. Have you found it difficult to "forgive yourself" after sinning against God and others? Where can you look in Scripture for assurance?
5. Take some time to search for the Scriptures that address your trial or temptation, and commit them to memory.

8

Sovereign Help When It's Hard to Forgive

"As for you, you meant evil against me,
but God meant it for good."
(Gen. 50:20)

We have all been hurt by other people. Some of us have been hurt very badly. What difference does believing in the sovereignty of God make in our response to this kind of treatment? The ability to forgive might not be the first thing that comes to mind when you consider this truth, but allow me to show you an example of how trust in the sovereignty of God can help you overcome the bitterness that may exist in your heart toward another person.

One of the most interesting characters in Scripture is Joseph.[1] He was one of twelve brothers and one of only two to be the issue of Jacob and his beloved wife Rachel. While many of us try to avoid

1 Joseph's story is found in Genesis 35–50.

partiality toward our children, Jacob didn't attempt to hide it. Joseph and Benjamin were clearly the favorites, and the other brothers were well aware of it. It didn't help that Jacob gave Joseph a multicolored coat, a very extravagant gift (think Louis Vuitton or Jean Paul Gaultier these days). It also didn't help that Joseph had dreams that were interpreted as his brothers' and his parents' paying homage to him. It does make you wonder about Joseph's judgment in sharing these dreams with his family. All these things together resulted in his brothers' absolutely hating him.

As the story progresses, the brothers saw an opportunity to get rid of Joseph. There was some thought of resorting to cold-blooded murder. Instead, they decided to sell him as a slave to traders who happened by. But what would they tell their dear father? They took Joseph's despised multicolored robe and dipped it in the blood of a goat that they had slaughtered in order to deceive their father. They presented the blood-soaked robe to Jacob, who concluded that Joseph had indeed been torn apart by a wild animal. He was as good as dead to Jacob and the brothers.

What happened to Joseph? It turns out that the traders sold him to Potiphar, the captain of Pharaoh's guard. He was a very prominent man in Egypt. Joseph served this man so well that Potiphar put him in charge of everything in his household. Unfortunately, as we saw in chapter 7, Potiphar's wife had her eye on Joseph, regularly made advances toward him, and eventually accused *him* of improper advances. Though the charges were false, Joseph was thrown into prison. But he prospered there as well. He was so trustworthy that the jailer put him in charge of the rest of the prisoners. While Joseph was there, God also enabled him to interpret the dreams of two of his fellow prisoners, predicting execution for one and vindication for the other. His interpretation was exactly right, and he asked the official who was exonerated to remember him when he was restored to his place at court.

Well, the official forgot about Joseph for two whole years, until Pharaoh had a dream that deeply disturbed him, *and then* the official remembered that Joseph had accurately interpreted his own dream. Pharaoh called Joseph to court, and God enabled him to interpret the dream, which predicted seven years of prosperity followed by seven years of famine. Joseph suggested that preparations be made for the years of famine by storing surplus grain during the years of prosperity. Pharaoh directed that preparations be made accordingly, and he put Joseph in charge of the plan! It happened just as God had revealed in the dream. The prosperous years were great, but the famine was very severe, and it extended throughout the region to the land of Canaan. Eventually, Egypt was the only place where grain could be found. Jacob sent his sons to Egypt to buy grain.

To shorten the story, eventually Joseph revealed himself to his brothers in a very emotional reunion. He graciously invited them to bring their families to Egypt and to enjoy the security that would now belong to them as part of Joseph's family. Of course, they would bring Joseph's father as well, for whom this reunion was like receiving someone back from the dead. Pharaoh was pleased to meet them and to welcome them, and he provided sufficient land for them to pasture their flocks and raise their families. And their worries about "food security" were over even though they were in the midst of a great famine.

One important area in which the brothers were not secure was their wondering when the day of reckoning would come for selling Joseph into slavery. Certainly, he would hold them accountable for what they had done to him. But when? The years passed, but they were still troubled by their consciences.

After many years, Jacob died. He had requested that he be buried back in the land of Canaan in the tomb of his father and his grandfather. Pharaoh granted permission for Joseph to travel there for this purpose. Lingering in the hearts of his brothers was still the question of when Joseph was going to settle things from the past. Now that their father was gone, wouldn't this be the time for him to get even? This is exactly what his brothers thought. The guilt of their transgression had haunted them all these years. The Scottish clergyman George Lawson describes what they might have imagined:

> Joseph now had them in his power. What if their brother, now so highly exalted above them, should make them feel the power of his arm in the infliction of vengeance? If a man find his enemy, will he let him go well away? If Joseph did not take advantage of his greatness to destroy or enslave them, was it to be expected that he would conceal their crimes from the people and the king of Egypt? Would they not be rendered so hateful to Pharaoh and to his people, that it would be difficult for them to make their escape out of that land into which they had sold their brother?[2]

Or was their anxiety based on the fact that they had been "caught"? We don't have to imagine what was going through their minds. They said, "It may be that Joseph will hate us and pay us back for all the evil that we did to him" (Gen. 50:15). They had to imagine that the

---

2 George Lawson, *The History of Joseph* (London: Banner of Truth Trust, 1972), 257.

payback would include being sold into slavery along with their wives and children. Now it would be Joseph's turn.

So the brothers were proactive and concocted a story. Here is what they said:

> So they sent a message to Joseph, saying, "Your father gave this command before he died: 'Say to Joseph, "Please forgive the transgression of your brothers and their sin, because they did evil to you."' And now, please forgive the transgression of the servants of the God of your father." Joseph wept when they spoke to him. (Gen. 50:16–17)

Certainly, Joseph wouldn't seek retribution for their evildoing if he knew that his late beloved father had been concerned about it, would he? When he heard their words, he didn't try to get to the bottom of the myth he had just been told. He didn't investigate by asking, "When did he tell you that?" or "If that was so important to him, why didn't he tell me?"

What was Joseph's reaction to their tale? He wept. The very suggestion that he was waiting to get even with his brothers until after Jacob died was unthinkable to him. But his brothers didn't know that until Joseph spoke these remarkable words: "'Do not fear, for am I in the place of God? As for you, you meant evil against me, but God meant it for good, to bring it about that many people should be kept alive, as they are today. So do not fear; I will provide for you and your little ones.' Thus he comforted them and spoke kindly to them" (Gen. 50:19–21). These are among the most gracious words ever spoken in the Bible. They are words of mercy and forgiveness. How was it possible for Joseph to be so kind to those who had been determined to get rid of him one way or another and settled on selling him into slavery? Fundamentally, he could do so because he was a man who believed in the sovereignty of God. In these words, we see several things that can help us when we are mistreated by others.

First, Joseph asked, "Am I in the place of God?" (v. 19). He was bluntly saying that "God is God and I'm not!" He acknowledged that it was the Lord's prerogative to deal with his brothers' sin. He didn't downplay their sin. He didn't say, "Oh, well, I knew you didn't mean anything by it." Neither did he say, "I brought it on myself through my dreams." No, he said, "As for you, you meant evil against me" (v. 20). There, he said it. What they had done to him was evil!

But the matter of that accountability for their evil was not up to Joseph but up to God. The Scriptures clearly teach that we are not to take matters into our own hands: "Repay no one evil for evil, but give thought to do what is honorable in the sight of all. If possible, so far as it depends on you, live peaceably with all. Beloved, never avenge yourselves, but leave it to the wrath of God, for it is written, 'Vengeance is mine, I will repay, says the Lord'" (Rom. 12:17–19). When someone sins against you, let there be no doubt that it is sin. But remember that the person is ultimately accountable to God, not you. Philip Ryken advises: "So if people do you wrong, forgive them, whether or not they ask for forgiveness. You cannot cancel their sin. Only God can do that, and He will only do it if they repent. But what you can do is set aside your own anger, bitterness, and resentment towards them."[3]

As we have already noted, God is sovereign in the exercise of all His attributes, and this includes His administration of justice. Do

3 Philip Graham Ryken, *When You Pray: Making the Lord's Prayer Your Own* (Wheaton, Ill.: Crossway, 2000), 141.

you believe it? Are you willing to trust His justice? Sadly, we often prefer our own justice to forgiveness. "Forgiving costs us our sense of justice. We all have this innate sense deep within our souls, but it has been perverted by our selfish sinful natures. We want to see 'justice' done, but the justice we envision satisfies our own interests."[4] It is always crucial to keep God's interests at the center of our assessment.

Second, Joseph recognized that the Lord was working out His plan *through* the evil perpetrated by his brothers: "As for you, you meant evil against me, but God meant it for good" (Gen. 50:20). That's right; Joseph could see that God meant *everything* for good, including his brothers' hatred, their selling him into slavery, the false accusations of Potiphar's wife, and those years in an Egyptian prison. What was the good? Joseph could look back and see that God had used everything that happened so that "many people should be kept alive" (v. 20). That is certainly a humble assessment of the result. It was more than "many"; it was the entire population of Egypt as well as the surrounding region!

This had been Joseph's assessment of the situation for a long time. The first words he had spoken to his brothers after he revealed his identity to them seventeen years earlier expressed the same sentiment:

> So Joseph said to his brothers, "Come near to me, please." And they came near. And he said, "I am your brother, Joseph, whom you sold into Egypt. And now do not be distressed or angry with yourselves because you sold me here, for *God sent me before you to preserve life*. For the famine has been in the land these two years,

---

4 Jerry Bridges, *The Practice of Godliness* (Carol Stream, Ill.: NavPress, 1996), 207–8.

> and there are yet five years in which there will be neither plowing nor harvest. And *God sent me before you* to preserve for you a remnant on earth, and to keep alive for you many survivors. *So it was not you who sent me here, but God.* He has made me a father to Pharaoh, and lord of all his house and ruler over all the land of Egypt." (Gen. 45:4–8, emphasis added)

He identified the fact that, humanly speaking, *they* had sold him into slavery, acknowledging their wrongdoing. They knew their sin, which explains why "they were dismayed at his presence" (v. 3). They were shocked, confused, and terrified all at once. But notice Joseph's clear recognition of the plan of God behind it all, to the point that he proclaimed, "So it was not you who sent me here, but God." There could not have been a clearer expression of Joseph's belief in the sovereignty of God.

> Joseph was taught by God to acknowledge and revere His providence in all that befell him. He saw the hand of God in his afflictions and saw goodness and mercy in them, and could cheerfully forgive those who were God's instruments in bringing him low. He saw the hand of God in his exaltation, and kept in view the end for which he was raised on high. He was not immoderately dejected by adversity, for he knew that his God would do him no hurt that would not be overruled for his good.[5]

Joseph knew that there was even more at stake than *his* good. It was not merely the members of his immediate family and the population

5 Lawson, *The History of Joseph*, 264.

of Egypt who were saved, but in preserving the family of the patriarchs, "the remnant" of the covenant line of promise would continue unbroken, eventually bringing forth the promised Messiah, through whom the ultimate blessing of forgiveness is found.

Joseph's belief in the sovereignty of God drained his heart of the need for vengeance or retribution. We can't *always* see how someone's sin against us is part of God's unfolding plan. But if we believe that He causes "all things [to] work together for good" (Rom. 8:28), how can we exclude anything, including being mistreated by others?

In the mystery of His providence, God used the most hateful deed of history for our salvation: "Men of Israel, hear these words: Jesus of Nazareth, a man attested to you by God with mighty works and wonders and signs that God did through him in your midst, as you yourselves know—this Jesus, delivered up according to the definite plan and foreknowledge of God, you crucified and killed by the hands of lawless men. God raised him up, loosing the pangs of death, because it was not possible for him to be held by it" (Acts 2:22–24). The fact that God *uses* evil deeds for His purpose does not absolve the perpetrators of responsibility, and His plan cannot be foiled. It was while Jesus was on the cross in the midst of His suffering that He said, "Father, forgive them, for they know not what they do" (Luke 23:34). Jesus knew the greater plan. He knew that He was going to Jerusalem not to be crowned king but to be crucified.

It is only when we believe in this greater plan that we can not only forgive but love our enemies, the power of which we hear in the countercultural words of Jesus in the Sermon on the Mount: "You have heard that it was said, 'You shall love your neighbor and hate your enemy.' But I say to you, Love your enemies and pray for those who persecute you" (Matt. 5:43–44).

Is it possible to "forgive and forget"? One of the most amazing prophetic statements concerning the blessings of the new covenant given to us in Christ is found in Jeremiah: "For I will forgive their iniquity, and I will remember their sin no more" (Jer. 31:34). These words are repeated in the New Testament, acknowledging their fulfillment in the ministry of Jesus (see Heb. 8:12). Yes, these words speak about God's mercy, but what does it mean when we are told that the Lord "will remember their sin no more"? How is this possible? Does the omniscient God somehow develop cosmic amnesia? Not at all.

In some cases when the Old Testament uses the word "remember," it is not merely a cognitive exercise. Rather, the remembrance is linked with action related to the person or object. For example, in Genesis 8:1, we are told: "But God *remembered* Noah and all the beasts and all the livestock that were with him in the ark. And God made a wind blow over the earth, and the waters subsided" (emphasis added). It is not as though God had *forgotten* that Noah and the creatures from all over the earth were in that stuffy ark; rather, the time had come for *action to be taken* to relieve them, which started with the slow elimination of the floodwaters from the earth. Similarly, when the cries of His enslaved people in Egypt rose to Him, we read, "And God heard their groaning, and *God remembered* his covenant with Abraham, with Isaac, and with Jacob" (Ex. 2:24, emphasis added). This time, the covenant with the patriarchs was to be the basis of the deliverance to follow. This helps us understand the promise that He "will remember their sin no more." The idea is that He will no longer remember our sins *for the action that they deserve: condemnation*. Because we have been forgiven through the atoning work of Jesus on the cross, "there is therefore now no condemnation for those who are in Christ Jesus" (Rom. 8:1).

This is the answer to those who would say that we have to "forgive *and forget*." There is not a "delete" button on our minds that we can press to eliminate what has been done to us. But even as God no longer *remembers* our sin in the sense that it leads to our judgment, so through the power of the Holy Spirit, and grounded in the forgiveness and mercy that we have received from Christ, the *remembrance* of someone's sin against us can be drained of the poisonous desire to "get even" or to do harm to that person in any way.

Living as a sovereigntist includes the great challenge of trusting God's plan even when people sin against us and mistreat us. Yes, He is using even this "for our good." Ask Him for the grace to forgive, even as you have been forgiven.

Mark of a Sovereigntist: Willingness to Forgive

Christians have often repeated the petition of the Lord's Prayer "and forgive us our debts, as we also have forgiven our debtors" (Matt. 6:12). As we ask our Father in heaven for forgiveness, it is presumed that we have also forgiven those who have sinned against us. Jesus told a parable that reveals the imperative of forgiveness.[6] He told us about a man who owed a massive debt[7] to a king in which he was inclined to sell the man, his wife, his children, and everything he owned, which still would not nearly pay off the debt. The man fell down before the king and pleaded for the opportunity to pay back the debt. Remarkably, the king was moved and forgave the entire debt!

---

6 The parable is found in Matthew 18:23–35, in response to Peter's question, "Lord, how often will my brother sin against me, and I forgive him? As many as seven times?" to which Jesus answered, "Seventy-seven times" (vv. 21–22).

7 Ten thousand talents; a single talent was equivalent to a laborer's wages for about twenty years.

The plot thickens when the same man, with a new lease on life, was approached by another man who owed him a microscopic amount compared to what he had been forgiven.[8] Was he magnanimous in light of the mercy he had received? No! He had the man thrown into prison. When the merciful king heard what the man had done, he brought him in and admonished him: "You wicked servant! I forgave you all that debt because you pleaded with me. And should not you have had mercy on your fellow servant, as I had mercy on you?" (18:32–33). He changed his mind and threw the man into prison.

What's the point? Have you ever begun to calculate how many sins you have committed against God and your fellow human beings? Have you ever thought about the spiritual debt you have accrued? Now think about how *merciful* God has been, "having forgiven us *all our trespasses*, by canceling the record of debt that stood against us with its legal demands. This he set aside, nailing it to the cross" (Col. 2:13–14, emphasis added). In Jesus Christ, He has forgiven *every* sin: past, present, and future. Compare that to the offenses that someone has committed against you. They are hurtful and painful, but compared to what you have been forgiven, they are like dust. Speaking of the king's actions toward the unmerciful man, Jesus concluded the parable with these words: "So also my heavenly Father will do to every one of you, if you do not forgive your brother from your heart" (Matt. 18:35). Those are stunning words, but if we *really* understand how much we have been forgiven, we will be ready to forgive others. Paul urged, "Be kind to one another, tenderhearted, forgiving one another, as God in Christ forgave you" (Eph. 4:32).

---

8 One hundred denarii; a single denarius was equivalent to a laborer's wages for a day's work.

For Further Reflection

1. Did Joseph's brothers ever "forget" the evil they had done to him?
2. Did Joseph ever "forget" what his brothers had done to him?
3. How did Joseph's belief in God's sovereignty make it possible for Joseph to forgive his brothers?
4. Did Joseph's forgiveness overlook the magnitude of the evil that his brothers had done to him?
5. Are you finding it difficult to forgive someone? How does trust in God's sovereign plan help you to forgive?

Part Four

THAT'S A GOOD QUESTION

9

If God Is Sovereign, Why Bother to Pray?

"People who catch the vision of this glorious sovereign God,
who has destined the prayers of His people to be a means
of executing His unspeakably wonderful decrees,
have a way of transforming the world."
—Douglas Kelly

A question that commonly arises related to this subject is this: "If God is sovereign, why bother to pray?" If He not only *knows* what is going to happen but has *determined* what is to be, why should we pray? Is this exercise worth the time and effort if it is not going to make any difference?

As we have already seen, an essential characteristic of sovereigntists is that they are obedient to the Sovereign. An important answer to the question "Why bother to pray?" is that we are *commanded* to pray. Conversation with the Lord is a blessed benefit of the redemption that we now have as adopted children of our Father in heaven. In fact, the words "Our Father in heaven" are the opening words of the prayer that Jesus taught His disciples (Matt. 6:9). Prayer begins with the acknowledgment that our Lord is in heaven and reigning over all. His presumption is that His followers will pray. In fact, shortly after the reminder in the Sermon on the Mount that His sheep do not need to be anxious about having enough clothing to wear or food to eat,[1] Jesus urges them: "Ask, and it will be given to you; seek, and you will find; knock, and it will be opened to you. For everyone who asks receives, and the one who seeks finds, and to the one who knocks it will be opened" (7:7–8).

If there was ever One who was in complete sync with the Father, it was the Son. If there was ever One who understood the glory and majesty of the Father, it was Jesus Christ. Yet His life was a life of prayer. We are told that Jesus rose "very early in the morning, [and] while it was still dark, he departed and went out to a desolate place, and there he prayed" (Mark 1:35). Luke reports, "In these days he went out to the mountain to pray, and all night he continued in prayer to God" (Luke 6:12).

Jesus was the perfect Son of God and walked in His Father's will without exception, and yet His life was marked by dependent prayer. Perhaps the most poignant example is His anguish in Gethsemane as He sought relief from the burden of our sin that He had come to bear, but His perfect response was, "Nevertheless, not as I will, but as you will" (Matt. 26:39).

How Does Prayer Fit into the Plan?

The Lord has ordained not only whatsoever will come to pass but also the *means* by which it will come to pass. Prayer is a secondary

1 Matthew 6:25–34.

means that He has ordained to accomplish His purpose. If I move a book from my bookshelf to my desk, I can say that the book's being on my desk is part of His plan but that the secondary means was the exercise of my arm to reach the book and my hand to grasp the book and place it on the desk. Similarly, prayer is a link in the chain of God's providence.

> In some extraordinary way, the unchanging, sovereign God, with an eternally defined purpose for His creatures, invites our input into the making of history. As we think about praying for the plan of God to come to pass in our lives and in the whole world, we can keep the right perspective if we hold together in our minds these two tremendous, Biblical truths. The first is that God has an all-encompassing plan and is utterly sovereign over all. The other is that human prayer really is effective in the supernatural realm.[2]

The better question would be, "If God *isn't* sovereign, why pray at all?" For the sovereigntist, God is in control of all things and is in the position to move mountains to accomplish His purpose through His people. If you do not believe in the sovereignty of God, how can you be sure, even if He is willing, that He is *able* to answer your prayers? Perhaps your prayer has touched an area in which God does *not* reign? The dilemma of a nonsovereign God and prayer is more difficult than belief in God's reign over all things.

Another question that arises is, "Does prayer change God?" Richard Pratt addresses this question well when he answers these

---

2 Douglas F. Kelly, *If God Already Knows, Why Pray?* (Brentwood, Tenn.: Wolgemuth & Hyatt, 1989), 60–61.

questions: "Do we try to change God through prayer? Are our requests intended to compel Him to act in ways He did not already intend? If God is unchanging, why do we bother to pray at all? To answer these questions, we must look at prayer from two vantage points. In one sense petitions certainly do not change God. In another sense, however, prayers are ordained by God Himself as a means of moving Him to action."[3] The short answer is that we can never change God or His plan, but He has ordained that our prayers are part of accomplishing that plan. Practically speaking, therefore, we can't say that a particular answer to prayer would have happened *had we not prayed*.

Yes, this is difficult for us to fathom, but it should humble us as we are given the privilege and the responsibility for our prayers to be part of God's plan. What is the takeaway?

Because God Is Sovereign, Pray Passionately

If we are convinced that God is working out His plan and also that He has ordained prayer as a secondary means to accomplish that plan, we should pray passionately. This is exactly why Jesus urged His disciples to pray with confidence: "And I tell you, ask, and it will be given to you; seek, and you will find; knock, and it will be opened to you" (Luke 11:9). The verbs are in the imperative mood, which gives the sense of "Ask! Seek! And knock!" There should be an intensity and even a desperation in our prayers. Unfortunately, this is often not the case with us. Prayer is a last resort rather than our first response. Someone once asked, "Is prayer your steering

---

3 Richard L. Pratt Jr., *Pray with Your Eyes Open: Looking at God, Ourselves, and Our Prayers* (Phillipsburg, N.J.: Presbyterian and Reformed, 1987), 107–8.

wheel or your spare tire?" Jesus encourages us to come boldly with our requests.

Not only are the verbs in the imperative mood, but they are in the present tense, which gives the sense of "Keep asking! Keep seeking! And keep knocking!" Jesus tells several parables that encourage us to be persistent in prayer. In fact, in the verses preceding these imperatives, Jesus tells the story of a man who visits a friend in the middle of the night. He pleads for food because another friend has arrived after a long journey, and he has nothing to give him to eat. No one likes to be disturbed in the middle of the night, so the request is declined. But that's not the end of the story. Jesus says, "Though he will not get up and give him anything because he is his friend, yet *because of his impudence he will rise and give him whatever he needs*" (v. 8, emphasis added). The idea behind the word translated "impudence" is "shameless persistence." It is important to note that the main point of the parable is not to highlight God's reluctance to answer prayer but to urge His people not to give up. *Keep asking, keep seeking, and keep knocking.*

What is the result? "For everyone who asks receives, and the one who seeks finds, and to the one who knocks it will be opened" (v. 10). What a promise! How could this be possible if God were not sovereign over all things? How could He even *know* what you are requesting, let alone answer?

Jesus continues: "What father among you, if his son asks for a fish, will instead of a fish give him a serpent; or if he asks for an egg, will give him a scorpion? If you then, who are evil, know how to give good gifts to your children, how much more will the heavenly Father give the Holy Spirit to those who ask him!" (vv. 11–13). These words may have brought about a little chuckle from Jesus' listeners because anyone who has paternal affection for his children will not give one of them something harmful instead of something good: a snake instead of a fish or a scorpion instead of an egg. The very thought of it makes me squirm! No, even as earthly fathers want the very best for their children, so your heavenly Father desires to give you good gifts, including the Holy Spirit, who is given to all who believe in Jesus.

It is also fair to surmise, though not explicitly stated, that if a child were to ask for a scorpion or a snake, a wise parent would not give it to him. Certainly, if your child asked you for something that you knew would be harmful, you would not comply with the request. In the same way, sometimes we ask the Lord for something that He knows would not be good for us or might even be harmful to us. You can be sure that the answer will be "no."

Or we ask for the right things at the wrong time. Suppose your five-year-old asks you for the keys to the car to take a little spin around the block. Of course, you would not hand over the keys but would explain that the time will come when he will be old enough to go through the steps necessary to obtain a driver's license. Similarly, our timing might be off in some of our prayer requests. A current "no" might be a "not yet." This takes wisdom to know which of these is the right answer. If it becomes clear that the answer is "no," that is the time to take your prayers in a different direction.

Douglas Kelly writes: "People who catch the vision of this glorious sovereign God, who has destined the prayers of His people to be a means of executing His unspeakably wonderful decrees, have a way of transforming the world. They have the assurance that the power of God Himself can be brought to bear."[4]

4 Kelly, *If God Already Knows, Why Pray?*, 64.

Be Willing to Accept God's Answer

A "no" to a prayer can be a means that God uses to direct our paths in life. I started out as a tuba performance major in college. That's right; I said "tuba performance." You would be surprised at how agile this gargantuan instrument can be. I was determined to prove to the world that the tuba was capable of far more than "oom-pah-pah." Actually, those who are knowledgeable about these things understand that the tuba claims only the "oom." The "pah-pah" is claimed by other instruments. I sought to accelerate my virtuosity by auditioning for the prestigious Curtis Institute in Philadelphia. The audition went very well, but the person who won the only position available was the prize student of the tuba professor. Then I decided to audition for the President's Own United States Marine Band in Washington, D.C. Once again, the audition went very well, but another person took the spot. I was unhappy and I was frustrated, but I later discovered that the Lord had closed these doors so that He might open another door into a life of service in ministry.[5] He *sovereignly* closed those doors and opened others. Please don't be discouraged if the answer has been "no" as you have sought a particular job or a relationship. When there is a closed door, keep your eyes alert to the provision of an open one.

A "no" answer is always the Lord's leading us according to His perfect will. Our Savior Himself experienced a "no" in the garden of Gethsemane. You recall that He asked the Father, "If it be possible, let this cup pass from me" (Matt. 26:39). He persisted three times in this prayer. Was there any other way? It was clear that there was no

5 God enabled me to continue using my musical gifts as an avocation through the Philly Pops and the Westminster Brass.

other way. Jesus humbly accepted this, saying, "Nevertheless, not as I will, but as you will" (v. 39).

Similarly, the Apostle Paul refers to a "thorn … in the flesh" (2 Cor. 12:7) that he asked the Lord to remove. Though the identity of this "thorn" is not definitively known, many scholars believe that it was a physical affliction of some kind.[6] He writes: "Three times I pleaded with the Lord about this, that it should leave me. But he said to me, 'My grace is sufficient for you, for my power is made perfect in weakness'" (vv. 8–9). Did Paul become bitter about this answer? No, he accepted the answer and went on to say: "Therefore I will boast all the more gladly of my weaknesses, so that the power of Christ may rest upon me. For the sake of Christ, then, I am content with weaknesses, insults, hardships, persecutions, and calamities. For when I am weak, then I am strong" (vv. 9–10). You will notice that he went on to include not only the "thorn … in the flesh," but a variety of hardships he experienced in his ministry. His perspective was to be content within the sovereign plan of God and to have faith that, even in this, the Lord's strength would sustain him. These are not the words of a stoic. No, this is the expression of the Apostle's confident faith in the living God.

Claim God's Promises

Because God is sovereign, He keeps His promises. One of the best prayer practices is to claim the promises of God. C.H. Spurgeon likened God's promises to a checkbook from "the Bank of Faith," comparing the promises of God to a bank check that needs to be personally endorsed before being cashed: "He is to take the promise,

---

6 Some have thought it to be a problem with Paul's eyesight.

and endorse it with his own name by personally receiving it as true. He is by faith to *accept* it as his own. This done, he must believingly *present* the promise as a man presents a cheque at the Counter of the Bank. He must plead it by prayer, expecting it to be fulfilled."[7] Spurgeon's point is that we should personally claim these promises or they remain like uncashed checks, their value never being realized. There are so many promises to be claimed that they cannot all be named at this point. But here are a few:

> Do not be anxious about anything, but in everything by prayer and supplication with thanksgiving let your requests be made known to God. And the peace of God, which surpasses all understanding, will guard your hearts and your minds in Christ Jesus. (Phil. 4:6–7)
>
> I can do all things through him who strengthens me. (v. 13)
>
> And my God will supply every need of yours according to his riches in glory in Christ Jesus. (v. 19)
>
> "I will never leave you nor forsake you." (Heb. 13:5)

These, together with hundreds of other promises, are truly a treasure of riches with which the Lord has blessed His people. But did you ever think about the fact that God could not possibly keep His promises if He weren't sovereign? We have asked that question

---

7 Charles H. Spurgeon, *The Cheque Book of the Bank of Faith* (London: Marshall, Morgan, and Scott, 1957), v.

throughout this book. When we, as humans, make promises to one another, we *hope* that we can keep them. Many times we do, but sometimes unexpected circumstances arise or, worse, we decide not to keep the promises. Because God is sovereign, no circumstance can thwart His commitment.

John Owen declares: "All the promises of God are true and faithful, and shall most certainly all of them be accomplished. His nature, his veracity, his unchangeableness, his omnipotency, do all contribute strength to this assertion."[8] God's willingness to keep His promises is unwavering. Why? Because He sovereignly bestows these gifts on His people when they ask, and "all the promises of God find their Yes in [Jesus Christ]. That is why it is through him that we utter our Amen to God for his glory" (2 Cor. 1:20). The gift of His Son is the greatest fulfilled promise of them all, and elsewhere Paul reminds us, "He who did not spare his own Son but gave him up for us all, how will he not also with him graciously give us all things?" (Rom. 8:32). The logicians would call this an argument from the greater to the lesser. For example, if I were willing to give you one hundred dollars (which I'm not!), certainly I would be willing to give you ten. The Father gave you His Son (the greater), and He is certainly willing to give you your request (the lesser). But we must always keep in mind, as in the prayers of Jesus, wanting the Father's will and not our will.

Mark of a Sovereigntist: Persistence

Jesus told several parables about prayer, but one of my favorites is the parable of the persistent widow (Luke 18:1–8). In this case, we

8 *The Works of John Owen*, vol. 11 (London: Banner of Truth, 1966), 233.

are informed that the specific reason that Jesus told the parable is to teach us that we "ought always to pray and not lose heart" (v. 1). We are introduced to a widow who kept coming to a judge, looking for justice, but he didn't want anything to do with her. She kept coming day after day to get a hearing. For the judge, every day was like Groundhog Day. He would come to work, and there she was. Finally, he'd had enough. He said, "Because this widow keeps bothering me, I will give her justice, so that she will not beat me down by her continual coming" (v. 5). He heard her case not for the sake of justice but so that he could get rid of her.

Jesus makes the point that God is nothing like that judge: "And will not God give justice to his elect, who cry to him day and night? Will he delay long over them? I tell you, he will give justice to them speedily" (vv. 7–8). God is our loving heavenly Father who hears and acts on behalf of His people. Not only is God not like the judge, but we are not like the widow. The widow was an unknown nobody to the judge. God's people are the "elect," the ones He chose from before the foundation of the world to be lovingly adopted as His children through faith in Jesus Christ. Jesus tells us, however, that we should resemble the widow in one way: her persistence. Don't give up until you are clear that what you are asking is not His will. Your Father is eager to hear and answer your prayers according to His will. Don't give up!

For Further Reflection

1. If God sovereignly determines what is to happen, why should we pray?
2. How does the fact of God's rule over all things encourage you to pray?

3. Are you willing to accept a "no" from God? Can you think of an example? How did you know that the answer was "no"?
4. Write down and share some of your favorite promises of God found in the Scriptures.

10

If God Is Sovereign, Why Bother to Share Your Faith?

"God did not teach us the reality of His rule
in order to give us an excuse for neglecting His orders."
—J.I. Packer

The sovereignty of God in the matter of salvation is controversial to many, but the Scriptures are clear that the identity of those who will be saved is ultimately God's choice. This is offensive to many because, they say, "it is not fair." As we saw in chapter 9, the Bible refers to those who are chosen by God as His "elect." His sovereignty in election is seen throughout Scripture. Of all who were alive in the ancient world at the time, God chose Abram, through whom He would establish a nation to worship and glorify Him. From all the nations of the earth, God chose Israel to be His people. Here is the rationale:

> "It was not because you were more in number than any other people that the LORD set his love on you and chose you, for you were the fewest of all peoples, but it is because the LORD loves you and is keeping the oath that he swore to your fathers, that the LORD has brought you out with a mighty hand and redeemed you from the house of slavery, from the hand of Pharaoh king of Egypt. Know therefore that the LORD your God is God, the faithful God who keeps covenant and steadfast love with those who love him and keep his commandments, to a thousand generations." (Deut. 7:7–9)

Notice the emphasis that the ground of God's choice was nothing about the people in particular but rather all about His sovereign love exercised in His plan and purpose.

When we look in the New Testament, we have the same language applied to those who have come to faith in Christ. In his letter to the Ephesians, the Apostle Paul writes:

> Blessed be the God and Father of our Lord Jesus Christ, who has blessed us in Christ with every spiritual blessing in the heavenly places, even as he *chose us in him* before the foundation of the world, that we should be holy and blameless before him. In *love he predestined us* for adoption to himself as sons through Jesus Christ, according to the purpose of his will, to the praise of his glorious grace, with which he has blessed us in the Beloved. (Eph. 1:3–6, emphasis added)

The origin of our salvation, and every blessing that comes with it, is in God's choice. This choice could not have ultimately been ours because it was "before the foundation of the world." In case we have any doubt about what he intends by this language, Paul adds, "In love he predestined us for adoption" and that this is "according to the purpose of his will." Our salvation finds its origin in God. R.C. Sproul observes: "The redemption of His people, the salvation of His church, my eternal salvation, these actions are not a postscript to the Divine activity. Instead, from the very foundation of the world, God had a sovereign plan to save a significant portion of the human race, and He moves heaven and earth to bring it to pass."[9]

Specifically, bringing all these blessings to pass required the mission of Jesus to come into the world and pay the penalty for the sins of the elect. This is why we are reminded that these blessings are "in Christ," that God chose us "in him," that we are predestined to adoption "through Jesus Christ," and that all are "in the Beloved."

Paul doesn't end there. He reemphasizes God's sovereign grace in our salvation by adding, "In him we have obtained an inheritance, having been predestined according to the purpose of him who works all things according to the counsel of his will, so that we who were the first to hope in Christ might be to the praise of his glory" (vv. 11–12). Again, the emphasis is on *His* purpose and *His* will.

Similarly, John focuses on this in the prologue to his gospel. After observing that many did not welcome Jesus, he adds, "But to all who did receive him, who believed in his name, he gave the right to become children of God, who were born, not of blood nor of the will of the flesh nor of the will of man, but of God" (John 1:12–13). John notes that there are those who do "receive" and "believe," but that the ultimate determining factor is not their will but God's. Here

9 R.C. Sproul, *The Purpose of God: An Exposition of Ephesians* (Fearn, Scotland: Christian Focus, 1994), 23.

we see that balance between human responsibility and God's sovereignty, but there is no doubt that the preeminent component is the will of God.

In His remarkable nighttime conversation with the inquiring Nicodemus, Jesus declares, "Truly, truly, I say to you, unless one is born again he cannot see the kingdom of God" (John 3:3). Interestingly, the very familiar language of being "born again" is the translation of the Greek words "born from above."[10] Leon Morris describes the contrast between human birth and the new life in Christ: "The new birth is always sheer miracle. All human initiative is ruled out. Men are born 'of God.' They can be born in no other way."[11] Similarly, you can hear the divine initiative in these words of Jesus: "All that the Father gives me will come to me" (6:37); "no one can come to me unless the Father who sent me draws him" (v. 44). As both contexts reveal, this does not dismiss the human response of faith but rather focuses on the divine origin of salvation.

Paul reminds his readers that faith itself is a gift from God. Returning to Paul's letter to the Ephesians, he tells his readers: "For by grace you have been saved through faith. And this is not your own doing; it is the gift of God, not a result of works, so that no one may boast" (Eph. 2:8–9). Even the faith that saves is "the gift of God." This is what grace is all about. Our salvation from start to finish is God's gift to sinners. The Puritan Samuel Bolton writes: "This leaves no room for human boasting. If there was anything of man's bringing, which was not of God's bestowing, though it were never so small, it

---

10 Greek *gennēthē anōthen*.

11 Leon Morris, *The Gospel according to John* (Grand Rapids, Mich.: Eerdmans, 1971), 101.

would overturn the nature of grace, and make that of works which is of grace."[12] If there were one iota of human merit or effort in our salvation, there would always be "room for boasting." But salvation is not merely a change of attitude or a change in the way we think; it is a total transformation, beginning with the heart.

When it comes to the decision to believe, the Scriptures teach that, yes, humans choose, but the divine choice comes first. People choose, but God chooses first. In the words of Jesus, "*You did not choose me, but I chose you* and appointed you that you should go and bear fruit and that your fruit should abide" (John 15:16, emphasis added).

After clearly articulating the doctrine of election in Romans, Paul anticipates objections to the preeminence of God's choice: "You will say to me then, 'Why does he still find fault? For who can resist his will?' But who are you, O man, to answer back to God? Will what is molded say to its molder, 'Why have you made me like this?' Has the potter no right over the clay, to make out of the same lump one vessel for honorable use and another for dishonorable use?" (Rom. 9:19–21). He writes, "So then he has mercy on whomever he wills, and he hardens whomever he wills" (v. 18). Do you hear what Paul is saying with regard to the matter of salvation? "God is God and I'm not."

So What's the Problem?

The argument goes that if God has ordained the number of those who will be saved, then why bother to share the gospel? The

12 Samuel Bolton, *The True Bounds of Christian Freedom* (Carlisle, Pa.: Banner of Truth, 1964), 94.

extreme expression of this view would go so far as to say that we shouldn't even bother to send missionaries to the "lost." If they are elect, God will save them without your help, thank you very much. There is no need for missionaries, preachers, or evangelists, according to this viewpoint. This is an unfortunate and inaccurate mischaracterization.

We must reiterate the biblical emphasis on human responsibility. Whenever one speaks of the sovereignty of God, as we have seen several times, it is important to be reminded of the Bible's emphasis on human responsibility. Being a sovereigntist is not to embrace a "let go and let God" attitude toward life but rather to live one's life in faith and obedience. Though Paul was completely secure in Christ and convinced of God's promise to bring him to his heavenly home, he was also convinced of his own responsibility to follow in faith. After assuring the Philippians of their security in Christ, he goes on to remind them to "work out your own salvation with fear and trembling, for it is God who works in you, both to will and to work for his good pleasure" (Phil. 2:12–13). He is saying that our salvation is a wonderful gift that is to be put to good use. We are called to yield to the Lord and walk in His ways through the power He provides. Paul describes his own attitude with the words of the runner moving toward the finish line: "press on," "straining forward," and "I press on toward the goal for the prize of the upward call of God in Christ Jesus" (3:12–14). The Bible teaches God's sovereignty and human responsibility. J.I. Packer relates Charles Spurgeon's words on the topic: "C. H. Spurgeon was once asked if he could reconcile these two truths to each other. 'I wouldn't try,' he replied; 'I never reconcile friends.' Friends?—yes, *friends*. This is the point we have to grasp. In the Bible, divine sovereignty and human responsibility are not enemies. They are not uneasy neighbors; they are not in an endless state of cold war with each other. They are *friends*, and they work together."[13]

Therefore, the answer to the question "Why bother to share your faith?" is the same as it was for the question "Why bother to pray?" God has ordained not only the end but the means to that end. He has ordained not only *who* will be saved but *how* they will be saved. If the end or goal is the salvation of the elect, the means ordained to bring them to that end is the preaching of the good news of Jesus Christ, who lived a perfect life, died for sin, and rose from the dead.

Paul describes it this way: "'Everyone who calls on the name of the Lord will be saved.' How then will they call on him in whom they have not believed? And how are they to believe in him of whom they have never heard? And how are they to hear without someone preaching? And how are they to preach unless they are sent? As it is written, 'How beautiful are the feet of those who preach the good news!'" (Rom. 10:13–15). This is the divine dynamic that the Lord has designed to occur in the salvation of the elect. He has entrusted the precious gospel of salvation to fallen yet redeemed people. This is truly an amazing privilege and responsibility for Christians. As we will see next, the sovereignty of God in salvation should motivate us to embrace this task.

Since God Is Sovereign, Share Your Faith Fervently

Since we know that there will be those who will respond to the gospel, we should be the most zealous in proclaiming the good news.

---

13 J.I. Packer, *Evangelism and the Sovereignty of God* (Downers Grove, Ill.: InterVarsity Press, 1961), 35–36.

I think you would agree that Paul was a sovereigntist, one who believed in the absolute sovereignty of God in all things, including salvation. Believing these truths didn't cause him to shrink from gospel preaching because God would save His elect. No, the man who most clearly articulated this truth was arguably the most passionate and effective missionary in the history of the church. Why? Because he knew that God's elect were out there and would respond to the good news. He is known to us through the narrative of his gospel exploits throughout the Mediterranean world. Luke, the chronicler of Paul's ministry in the book of Acts, gives an important note after the remarkable response of the whole city of Pisidian Antioch to the gospel. He tells us that "as many as were appointed to eternal life believed" (Acts 13:48). The analysis of their success did not focus on their human effort. Luke doesn't write, "Paul was really on fire today!" Their proclamation of the gospel was made effective when joined with the transforming power of the Spirit in the hearts of the elect, who were among the listeners.

The greatest evangelists in history were sovereigntists who believed that the Lord would use their proclamation of the gospel to bring people to faith in Jesus. This includes John Calvin, who was one of the most prolific church planters in history. John Starke reinforces this point:

> By 1555, Calvin and his Geneva supporters had planted five churches in France. Four years later, they had planted 100 churches in France. By 1562, Calvin's Geneva, with the help of some of their sister cities, had planted more than 2,000 churches in France. Calvin was the leading church planter in Europe. He led the way in every part of the process: he trained, assessed, sent,

> counseled, corresponded with, and prayed for the missionaries and church planters he sent.[14]

Calvin himself contradicted the caricatures that suggest that those who believe in election should merely sit on the sidelines and let God save whom He will save. No, he knew that God would use the faithful scattering of the seed of the gospel to bring about a great harvest.

Closet Sovereigntists?

When it comes to evangelism, I am convinced that *everyone* is a sovereigntist. While many would deny this, my experience tells me that even the skeptics are "closet sovereigntists." Why do I say this? I have been involved in innumerable evangelistic efforts throughout the decades with believers from diverse theological backgrounds. In every one of these efforts, without exception, whether it was an upcoming evangelistic service or visitation outreach, the prayers beforehand were always the same: "Dear Lord, please open their hearts to understand and receive the good news." In praying that the Lord would "open their hearts," those who would share their faith recognized that ultimately the "deciding" factor was not the ability of a person to articulate the gospel or the "reasonableness" of the recipient but the Spirit's work to open a person's heart to understand and believe. I have found no exceptions to the recognition of God's sovereign work in this way.

---

14 John Starke, "John Calvin, Missionary and Church Planter," The Gospel Coalition, November 27, 2012, https://www.thegospelcoalition.org/article/john-calvin-missionary-and-church-planter/.

Packer makes the same point: "The situation is not what it seems to be. For it is not true that some Christians believe in divine sovereignty while others hold an opposite view. What is true is that all Christians believe in divine sovereignty, but some are not aware that they do, and mistakenly imagine and insist that they reject it."[15] One of the clearest evidences of this "closet conviction" is the prayer meeting before the evangelistic outreach.

> Christ's command means that we all should be devoting all our resources of ingenuity and enterprise to the task of making the gospel known in every possible way to every possible person. Unconcern and inaction with regard to evangelism are always, therefore, inexcusable. And the doctrine of divine sovereignty would be grossly misapplied if we should invoke it in such a way as to lessen the urgency, and immediacy, and priority, and binding constraint of evangelistic imperative. God did not teach us the reality of His rule in order to give us an excuse for neglecting His orders.[16]

Since God Is Sovereign, Pray for Those You Know

Someone put it well in saying, "Before you talk to people about God, you should talk to God about people." Jack Miller, one of my professors at Westminster Seminary, helped us understand that *everyone* in the church needs to be involved in evangelistic outreach. Jack himself was involved in everything from global missions to street preaching. But it was Jack who reminded us that prayer is the most important

---

15 Packer, *Evangelism and the Sovereignty of God*, 16.
16 Packer, *Evangelism and the Sovereignty of God*, 33–34.

part of the evangelistic endeavor. Not if but since it is God who changes hearts of stone into hearts of flesh, we must be diligent in prayer for those who do not yet know the Lord. Though we must engage in creative ways to reach the lost, our ultimate dependence is on God and not the means. Packer would agree: "When you pray for unconverted people, you do so on the assumption that it is in God's power to bring them to faith. You entreat Him to do that very thing, and your confidence in asking rests upon the certainty that He is able to do what you ask. And so indeed He is."[17]

Sometimes all you can do is pray. Sometimes when we seek to reach a loved one or a friend, our efforts to talk to men about God give way to talking to God about men. As I mentioned in chapter 6, my wife was raised by a gracious and loving aunt. After her husband died, she met a man named Sonny. He was a handsome man with flowing white hair and piercing blue eyes. He was a tough guy and a long-haul truck driver for a farm-equipment manufacturer. Barb's aunt and Sonny married. From the very beginning of their relationship, Barb and I were looking for an opportunity to speak to him about the Lord. Whenever the subject came up, he said: "I know all about that. I am the son of a Mennonite preacher, and I heard all that and want nothing to do with it." This was the response whenever the subject was broached. Barb and I knew that prayer was our only hope; our exclusive strategy became one of "speaking to God about Sonny."

Years passed, and one Christmas morning I was sitting with Sonny as we awaited the call to Christmas dinner. He looked up at me with his customary cigarette in one hand and a cup of coffee in the other and said, "Tim, I have something I need to tell you." I said,

17 Packer, *Evangelism and the Sovereignty of God*, 15.

"OK." He said, "This is my first Christmas with Jesus in my heart." Even though we had been praying for this exact thing, his comment was jarring to me, and I almost let it pass. I could hardly believe my ears, so I asked him, "What did you say?" This time tears were running down his cheeks, and he repeated, "This is my first Christmas with Jesus in my heart." I asked, "What happened?" What I really meant was, "How did this happen?" He said: "You know that I have had some health problems recently, and I had to go for an MRI. While I was confined in the testing apparatus, I had a picture of myself in my own coffin, and I knew I wasn't ready to die. Then all the verses that I had learned as the son of a Mennonite preacher came flooding into my mind, and I trusted in Jesus." Needless to say, believers in the family rejoiced together with the angels in heaven. A few months later, Barb and I had the joy of attending a worship service where Sonny joined the church by profession of faith. It turns out that we weren't the only ones who had been praying for Sonny. His believing siblings surrounded him in tears, and his brother, Juny (for "Junior"), said, "The prodigal has come home."

The lesson for me is "Never give up on anyone." I misspoke above when I said that "prayer was our only hope." Prayer is never the last resort, but as Jack Miller said, it is the most important thing. Prayer for another person is evidence of God's grace toward that person. Douglas Kelly reminds us, "Whatever it is that prompts us to come to Him, the fact is that God Himself has ordained that these prayers of His people begin to release predestined blessings which would not have flowed down at all had the prayers not occurred."[18]

---

18 Douglas F. Kelly, *If God Already Knows, Why Pray?* (Brentwood, Tenn.: Wolgemuth & Hyatt, 1989), 64.

Mark of the Sovereigntist: Love

John wrote, "For God so loved the world, that he gave his only Son, that whoever believes in him should not perish but have eternal life" (John 3:16). The motivation for sending Jesus into the world was love. When Jesus saw the people who gathered around Him, "he had compassion for them, because they were harassed and helpless, like sheep without a shepherd" (Matt. 9:36). The first aspect of the fruit of the Spirit recorded by Paul is "love" (Gal. 5:22–23). Francis Schaeffer called love "the mark of the Christian."[19] The second great commandment is "You shall love your neighbor as yourself" (Mark 12:31). What better way is there to love our neighbor than to share the best news that we have ever heard? We recognize that *every* person, though sinful, is made in the image of God and needs the gospel to be reconciled to Him by faith in Jesus. When we are moved by the plight of those who don't know the Lord, "the love of Christ controls us," as Paul expresses it (2 Cor. 5:14).

Reformed people are often thought to be austere and even "the frozen chosen." This should not be the case. John Piper states: "Love is the overflow and expansion of joy in God, which gladly meets the needs of others. It is first a deeply satisfying experience of the fullness of God's grace, and then a doubly satisfying experience of extending this joy in God to another person."[20] Sovereigntists care for lost people, realizing that God's plan includes them in reaching others.

---

19 See his book of the same name: Francis Schaeffer, *Mark of the Christian* (Downers Grove, Ill.: InterVarsity Press, 1970).

20 John Piper, *The Dangerous Duty of Delight* (Colorado Springs, Colo.: Multnomah, 2001), 44–45.

For Further Reflection

1. Why is it wrong to use God's sovereignty in salvation as an excuse for failing to share your faith?
2. Why should God's sovereignty in salvation motivate us to share our faith?
3. What is an appropriate prayer before you share the gospel? Make a list of people for whom you are concerned and ask the Lord: (a) to open their hearts to receive the good news and (b) for an opportunity to share the good news with them.
4. Are you "moved" in your heart as you consider the plight of lost people? Ask the Lord to give you a loving and winsome heart for those who do not know Jesus.

Conclusion

I hope that reading these pages has encouraged you to join the happy ranks of the sovereigntists, as I have sought to help you understand the biblical principles of God's sovereignty and the blessed implications of anchoring one's life in these principles through the various seasons through which we pass. Anchoring your life in the truth of God's sovereignty is nothing less than anchoring your life in God Himself. Being a sovereigntist recognizes not merely a general affirmation of God's rule but His reign over all things all the time. As I conclude, I would like to return to the eighth chapter of the book of Romans, where we began our study. We saw in chapter 2 above that Paul made the absolute affirmation that "all things work together for good, for those who are called according to his purpose" (Rom. 8:28)—not *some* things or *most* things, but *all* things. We noted that this could not possibly be true unless God is absolutely sovereign over everything.

As we turn to the concluding few verses of the chapter, the Apostle Paul makes another absolute statement that can be affirmed only if God is sovereign.[1] The central thought of Romans 8:38–39 is that

1 I must note that several of the thoughts in this chapter were inspired by Roger R. Nicole, "Optimism and God's Sovereignty," in *Our Sovereign God: Knowing and Serving the Lord of All*, ed. James Montgomery Boice (Phillipsburg, N.J.: P&R, 2023), 155–62.

nothing can separate us from God's love in Christ. Again, not *some* things or *certain* things, but *nothing* can separate us from His love:

> For I am sure that neither death nor life, nor angels nor rulers, nor things present nor things to come, nor powers, nor height nor depth, nor anything else in all creation, will be able to separate us from the love of God in Christ Jesus our Lord.

In outlining the potential disrupters of this love, Paul lists "death." That's right; death itself cannot disconnect us from the love of God. Of death, Roger Nicole writes:

> It separates those who die from their labors, belongings, and activities. It separates them from the fulfillment of their careers. It separates those who remain from their fellowship, company, and presence. When death has spoken there is no return. In that sense, death is the king of fears; it is the emperor of separators.[2]

Paul is not saying that we will not die. He is saying that in our death, though we are separated from life and loved ones in this world, we are not separated from His love. How is that possible? It is possible only because Jesus took the curse of death that we deserve upon Himself. The curse of death is not merely cessation of our physical existence but the eternal penalty due to our sins. Jesus bore this curse for us, as Paul writes: "Christ redeemed us from the curse of the law by becoming a curse for us—for it is written, 'Cursed is everyone who is hanged on a tree'" (Gal. 3:13). This is why he can

2 Nicole, 157.

say that though believers die, "to be absent from the body [is] to be at home with the Lord" (2 Cor. 5:8, NASB). Though we might fear the potential pain and suffering of dying, we no longer need to fear death itself because "it is a climactic bridge that leads us into a firmer and fuller fellowship with God than anything we have known in the days of our flesh."[3] For this reason, believers do not "grieve as others do who have no hope" (1 Thess. 4:13). No, death cannot separate us from God's love in Christ because His gracious and sovereign plan for us does not end at death.

Next on the list of potential separators is "life." "Neither death nor life" can "separate us from the love of God in Christ Jesus our Lord" (Rom. 8:38–39). How in the world can "life" potentially separate us from the love of God? This can be thought of in two ways. First, *our perception* of God's loving care can be threatened when we experience some of the hardships of life that come our way and that we have spoken of in this book, such as loss, grief, relational disintegration, illness, and suffering. When bad things happen, we can sometimes question God's love for us, adding a "daisy" to our theology: "He loves me, He loves me not." But Paul's statement reinforces the fact that not only do "all things work together for good" for those who love God (v. 28), but God's love for them is unchangeable and immutable.

This leads to the second thought about "life" separating us from the love of God. Nicole summarizes it this way: "Is it possible that after I have been the object of his loving care and after I have turned to him in response to the invitation of his grace, I may so persist in my iniquity, so harming myself in my unbelief, so

---

3 Nicole, 158.

dishonoring his name, that God will say, 'I am sick and tired of you; I don't want you in my heaven. You are not worthy to be received in the everlasting courts.'"[4] The answer is that God is *the* Good Shepherd, and He seeks out His stray sheep. The Lord brought wayward David back to himself through the words of Nathan the prophet. Didn't Jesus Himself seek out Simon Peter in Galilee to restore him after his three denials? Didn't the Prodigal Son come to himself after his life of debauchery and blowing his inheritance? God does not allow His children to be ultimately lost. He seeks them, finds them, and brings them home from the darkness of despair and the shadows of sin.

This truth is not intended to lead to a free pass to sin. No, it is designed to comfort the struggling, penitent sinner in the realization that God hasn't forsaken him. Jesus could not have put it more clearly than in John's gospel when He said: "My sheep hear my voice, and I know them, and they follow me. I give them eternal life, and they will never perish, and no one will snatch them out of my hand. My Father, who has given them to me, is greater than all, and no one is able to snatch them out of the Father's hand" (John 10:27–29). Because God is sovereign, no dimension of "life" can separate the believer from His love.

In addition to life and death, Paul covers everything and anything else that might separate us from the love of God, whether natural ("anything else in all creation") or supernatural (principalities and "powers"), whether in the dimension of space ("height nor depth") or in the dimension of time ("things present nor things to come") (Rom. 8:38–39). *Nothing at all* can separate us from the love

4 Nicole, 160.

of God in Christ Jesus. This absolute confidence can be ours only if God is Lord of all.

A Final Absolute

Romans 8 contains one more important absolute, which is actually the foundation for the rest. It is found in the very first verse of the chapter: "There is therefore now no condemnation for those who are in Christ Jesus." What a statement! *No* condemnation! Condemnation is what we deserve because of our sins, but God has answered our need with the gift of His Son, who took our condemnation upon Himself. This is the basis not only of every promise in this chapter but of *all* of God's promises: "All the promises of God find their Yes in him. That is why it is through him that we utter our Amen to God for his glory" (2 Cor. 1:20). For the sovereigntist, therefore, God receives all the glory: "Not to us, O LORD, not to us, but to your name give glory, for the sake of your steadfast love and your faithfulness!" (Ps. 115:1).

> Oh, the depth of the riches and wisdom and knowledge of God! How unsearchable are his judgments and how inscrutable his ways!
>
> > "For who has known the mind of the Lord,
> > or who has been his counselor?"
> > "Or who has given a gift to him
> > that he might be repaid?"
>
> For from him and through him and to him are all things. To him be glory forever. Amen. (Rom. 11:33–36)

Scripture Index

About the Author

Dr. Timothy Z. Witmer retired in 2021 after serving forty-two years in pastoral ministry in the Presbyterian Church in America. He was on the faculty of Westminster Theological Seminary in Philadelphia for twenty years, where he served as professor and coordinator of the Department of Practical Theology. Upon his retirement, he was designated professor emeritus.

He attended West Chester University (B.A.), where he was recognized as Distinguished Alumnus in 2013, Westminster Theological Seminary (M.Div.), and Reformed Theological Seminary (D.Min.).

He is author of *The Shepherd Leader*, *The Shepherd Leader at Home*, and *Mindscape: What to Think About Instead of Worrying* and editor of *The Shepherd's Toolbox.* He is a regular contributor to *Tabletalk* and is the founder of Shepherd Leader Ministries, which assists churches in developing effective shepherding care for their congregations.

He and his wife, Barbara, have been married for more than fifty years. They have been blessed with three grown children and eight grandchildren. As an avocation, Dr. Witmer performed with the Westminster Brass for more than forty years.